Remembering Lake Quinsigamond

From Steamboats to White City

Michael P. Perna, Jr.

Remembering
Lake Quinsigamond

From Steamboats to White City

Chandler House Press
Worcester, Massachusetts

Remembering Lake Quinsigamond: From Steamboats to White City

Copyright 1998 by Michael P. Perna, Jr.

ISBN 1-886284-02-4
Library of Congress Catalog Card Number 97-60311
First Edition
ABCDEFGHIJK

Published by

Chandler House Press

335 Chandler Street, Worcester, MA 01602 USA
(800) 642-6657 • (508) 756-9425 Fax
www.tatnuck.com

President
Lawrence J. Abramoff

Publisher/Editor-in-Chief
Richard J. Staron

Vice President of Sales
Irene S. Bergman

Editorial/Production Manager
Jennifer J. Goguen

Book & Cover Design
Janet Amorello

Cover Photo
Nash Studio

Dedicated to Sandy

TABLE OF CONTENTS

ACKNOWLEDGMENTS

A book of this type, by its very nature, would have been impossible to write without the assistance of many, many people. I obtained a great deal of information through personal interviews, some local, and others as far away as Florida, Michigan, New York, and Connecticut. I am grateful to each and every person who helped me tell this story. I can't hope to name everyone that shared memories and provided information, but I must acknowledge the following people who are "co-authors" of this work, so to speak.

I offer special thanks to members of the Cumming family, especially the late Ms. Isabelle Massei and Ms. Janet Esip of Shrewsbury, MA and their brother John Cumming of Mt. Pleasant, Michigan for his gracious permission to use parts of his written remembrances of White City and Lincoln Park. Mrs. Barbara (Burns) Caron and the late Mrs. Ruth Burns, daughter and widow, respectively, of the late Kenneth Burns, told me about the history of crew racing at the lake. Kenneth Trinder and the late August "Gus" Moalli were kind enough to share their stories about their experiences at the lake. John Dunn, Mr. Joseph "Pony" Lucier, and the late Mrs. Lucier provided wonderful details about White City.

Mrs. Jacob Young of Worcester, MA and Mrs. Judith Godin of Delray Beach, Florida were immensely helpful in furnishing details about Tatassit Beach and their late brother and uncle, respectively, Felix Pollet. Mr. Leon King and the Mulcahy family graciously let me tour Tatassit Beach and Sunset Beach. Mr. Ronald Bigelow of Boylston, MA was instrumental in supplying photos and information about his great grand-father Horace Bigelow and his Lake Quinsigamond interests. Albert "Lovey" Garganigo of Shrewsbury provided a wealth of information about his family's various activities at the lake. Roscoe "Rockie" Blunt shared much of what he has collected about the lake over the years. I would also like to thank my friends who supplied inspiration and guidance during the sometimes trying process of writing this book: John O'Toole, Mark Savolis, Robert Cormier, the late Alexander Lebeaux, and of course Michael Paika, whose enthusiasm for anything to do with the history of Lake Quinsigamond is contagious.

In addition, many people at the Worcester Public Library, the Worcester Historical Museum, the American Antiquarian Society, and the Goddard Library at Clark University were all very helpful in assisting me in my efforts and I thank them all.

Most importantly, I must thank my publisher Larry Abramoff and his able staff at the Tatnuck Bookseller Marketplace, especially Jennifer Goguen, without whom this book would never have been possible.

Finally, I must acknowledge the support and patience of my family during this endeavor: my wife Sandy, my sons Richard and Nicholas, and my parents Mr. and Mrs. Michael Perna, Sr.

Starting in 1857, when the first college regatta was held on Lake Quinsigamond, the lake and surrounding area became a focal point for the recreational pursuits of the local citizenry. Since the idea of leisure time was coming into vogue in the late 1870s, a great period of development began at the lake.

Steamboats traversed the lake's crystal waters; picnic groves, boathouses, and social clubs began to dot the shores; hotels were built to cater to the needs of vacationers eager to "take the air" at the lake. A narrow-gauge steam railroad, nicknamed the "Dummy," (a name coined because the locomotives were disguised to look like horsecars so they would not frighten the horses) carried passengers from downtown Worcester to see the sights. Amusement parks soon followed: Bigelow's Grove, Lincoln Park, the "Oval," and so on, culminating with the grand opening of the extravagant White City amusement park in 1905.

In the ensuing decades, thousands upon thousands of people, from the rich and famous to the average working class family, visited the lake and its attractions. A visit to Lake Quinsigamond was an exciting adventure for young and old alike.

This book tells the story of Lake Quinsigamond from the early boat races to the heyday of the amusement parks. It is a story that reaches into the not-so-distant past and surfaces in the present. I hope that you enjoy your visit to the lake as you read *Remembering Lake Quinsigamond: From Steamboats to White City.* Here are a few of the prominent personalities you will encounter in the pages of this book.

HORACE H. BIGELOW was a successful and well known businessman who made his fortune in manufacturing before he became involved in real estate development. In 1881, he bought a roller skating rink and installed an arc of electric lights; electricity was one of his primary interests. Then, in 1905, his dream to construct a giant amusement park at Lake Quinsigamond came to fruition. The White City amusement park opened on June 18, 1905. It was immensely popular and glittered with plenty of electric lights. Bigelow lived long enough to see his dream become a reality, but died in 1911, only six years after the White City amusement park opened. Its many attractions included "Shoot-the-Chutes," "Circle Swings," a dance hall, a fun house, a roller coaster, steamboats, games, concessions, and many special attractions. The White City amusement park closed 55 years later, on Labor Day 1960.

KENNETH F. BURNS won every crew race he competed in from 1922 to 1925. Burns, who later became chief of the Shrewsbury police department, revived crew racing at the lake by starting a boys' crew team at Shrewsbury High School in 1937. His team was very successful and his efforts helped attract various competitions to the lake: the Middle States Regatta in 1950, the National Regatta in 1951, and the Olympic trials in 1952. His family continued the tradition of coaching crew teams at the lake: both his daughter Barbara Caron and his granddaughter Pamela Krause coached teams at Shrewsbury High School. Burns passed away in 1982.

JESSE JOHNSON COBURN was a forty-niner in the California gold rush before he returned to Worcester and worked in the scrap metal business. He built the Quinsigamond House Hotel on the shore of the lake in 1867 and began running steamboats up and down it soon after. Then he bought more land around the lake and opened Lincoln Park as the lake's first amusement park, which featured a carousel, a bowling alley, a theater, and steamboat rides, among various attractions. Coburn was instrumental in organizing the construction of a railroad to quickly transport people to and from the growing resort area at the lake. By 1873, the Worcester and Shrewsbury Railroad (W&SRR), also known as the "Dummy" railroad, was opened for business. Within five years the railroad was thriving and more cars were added. In 1879, Coburn was indicted for his negligence in a fatal steamboat incident and died shortly after in 1886 at age fifty-three. All of his lake property was sold to Horace H. Bigelow except for his boat rental business, which he gave to his son, Alvarado Alonzo Coburn.

FELIX POLLET opened Tatassit Bathing Beach in 1928, inspired by the activity at nearby Sunset Beach. Eleven years earlier, at age seventeen, he owned a tire store; in 1938, he was reportedly the first person to come up with the idea of renting beach chairs on Miami Beach; years later, he was one of the last Americans to leave Cuba after Fidel Castro came to power. At Tatassit Beach, Pollet offered recreation and excitement to beach-goers with rides, concessions, and a nightclub called the Hi-Hat.

Michael P. Perna, Jr.
& Jennifer J. Goguen

A. A. Coburn ❧ Boat Builder

**EVERY DESCRIPTION IN STOCK
AND BUILT TO ORDER.**

BOATS AND CANOES

**PARTY BOATS, ADIRONDACKS,
ENGLISH RANDANS,
CANADIAN CANOES, ETC.**

A. A. Coburn's Boat Liveries
············· THE FINEST IN NEW ENGLAND ·············

One at Lincoln Park, Lake Quinsigamond, consisting of over one hundred Boats and Canoes, supplied with latest improvements in Oar Locks, Spoon Oars, Cushions, Etc. The other, at Lake Whalom, just outside the city of Fitchburg, at one of the finest picnic grounds in New England, consisting of thirty-five Boats, all new; one fine 40-ft. Steam Launch (new), all equipped in first-class shape. . ☞ Electric Cars connect with this Park every twenty minutes.

QUINSIGAMOND LAKE STEAMBOAT CO.

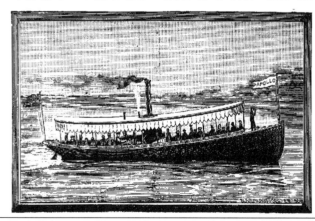

Steamers run regularly to all
points on ↯↯↯↯↯↯↯↯↯↯↯↯
LAKE
QUINSIGAMOND. ⚑

STEAMBOATS CHARTERED FOR
PRIVATE PARTIES BY THE
HOUR OR DAY.

IRVING E. BIGELOW, Treasurer,

Advertisement from Picturesque Views on & Adjacent to the Routes of the Worcester Consolidated Street Railway and at Lake Quinsigamond, 1898 (reprinted with permission from the Worcester Public Library)

The steamboats that once traveled up and down Long Pond, later known as Lake Quinsigamond, tell a story of the lake's vanished past. These steamers are described as "miniature things of beauty and a means of pleasure for the many" in a pamphlet entitled *Pleasure Resorts in Worcester County*, published in 1877.

Steamboats became quite popular at the lake and ranged in size from short and tubby to long and sleek. Some steamers, like the *Addie*, were side wheelers, while others used stern drive. The steamboats that once cruised the shores of Lake Quinsigamond include *Venus, Apollo, Parole, Dauntless, Dewey, Meteor, Uncle Sam, Tatassit, Col. Isaac Davis*, and *Mary Gertrude*. They sailed primarily on the southern half of the lake because they could not fit under the small causeway that spanned the lake prior to the existing Route 9 bridge. However, some boats had adjustable smokestacks which allowed them to fit under it. The steamboat docks were located in the area of Lincoln Park. The *Pleasure Resorts in Worcester County* pamphlet provides an excellent account of early steamboat traffic on the lake:

> *...boating at the lake seems to have successfully culminated in the line of S. E. Harthan's steamers, which ply about Quinsigamond. Steamboating on Worcester waters began in 1847, when for a brief season a small steam launch plied now and then about the lake. Several attempts in later years at steamboating were only indifferently successful and temporary, but in 1847 Mr. Harthan, taking advantage of the appreciation and popularity of Quinsigamond, which then was becoming manifest, placed on the waters his "Little Favorite," a small launch, and soon added his handsome and commodious side-wheeler, the "Addie." The success of the first season's steamboating was satisfactory to Mr. Harthan, and on the following summer he catered yet more extensively to those in this vicinity desiring to take a sea voyage at home. The present is the fourth season of Mr. Harthan's*

> *steamboat business on Quinsigamond, and the extent and success of his undertaking is attested by the liberal patronage of the public and the excellent and accommodating management of the proprietor. The boats of the Lake Quinsigamond line of steamers now number two, the "Little Favorite" having been disposed of to a private party, is still skipping over the waters, but no longer accommodates the public, though the lively little craft is viewed with much interest and admiration by visitors at the lake, as in contrast with the larger "Addie" and "Zephyr" it marks the beginning and growth of navigation on our inland sea.*

> *The "Addie" is a "side-wheeler," fifty-two feet long and sixteen wide over guards. It is furnished with a twenty-five horse power, two cylinder engine and vertical boiler, and easily and safely accommodates one hundred and seventy-five passengers, while as many as two hundred and over have been carried with no apparent danger or difficulty. The boat is tastefully painted and prettily ornamented, and as it glides over the water presents a charming sight, and leaves a real "wake" which well imitates that of a sound or river boat. The "Zephyr" is a handsome steam launch which Mr. Harthan placed upon the lake the present season. In size it is thirty feet by eight, and well carries fifty passengers. Both boats are finished inside in ash and black walnut with silver trimmings, and in their appointments and finishing are more stable and elegant than the average craft of their like. The boats are of Mr. Harthan's own make, and constructed with especial reference to the locality in which they were to be used. The officers and crews of the boats are courteous gentlemen well acquainted with and well suited to their business. With such fine steamers it might be expected that the lake would afford a fine course for their voyages, and a trip on either the "Addie" or the "Zephyr" will not disappoint the expectation.*

A system of colored flags at the boat landings indicated to the steamboat captain if there were passengers waiting to board at that particular place. (photo, Picturesque Worcester, 1895)

The steamboat landing is at the south-east corner of Quinsigamond Grove, or Lincoln Park as it is now more commonly called. Here a cute little wharf with pleasant seats under the shade of neighboring trees has been erected, and from this point at every hour during the pleasant summer days and moonlight evenings the captain's "all aboard" announces the "clearing" of one of the steamers.

Steaming out from the landing, the steamers steer for the center of the lake, leaving the fleets of small boats on the starboard, Bigelow's Grove on the port and Lincoln Park, the Quinsigamond House and fine view over the causeway and up the lake to the north at the stern.[1]

The pamphlet continues, describing the route taken by the steamers and the stops they made at various points around the south end of the lake. In a 1968 *Worcester Sunday Telegram* interview, Horace H. Bigelow, a grandson of the famous H. H. Bigelow who was so instrumental in developing the lake area, explained that a system of colored flags at various landings indicated to the steamboat captain if there were passengers waiting to board at that particular place. A red pennant signified passengers waiting to go down the lake; a yellow pennant signified passengers waiting to go up the lake.[2] The *Pleasure Resorts in Worcester County* narrative continues, describing a steamer's return voyage:

On the return trip the course steered gives the passengers a sight a trifle different from that on the outward voyage, and when the steamer is again moored at its landing during an hour's sail the pleasure seeker has enjoyed one of the grandest natural panoramas imaginable, and has avowed his twenty-five cents well invested. Besides, the hourly trips of the boats give one an opportunity to

spend a short time, or an afternoon, or even a day at either of the resorts along the lake shore.

The pleasure of the voyage is well attested by the fact that the boats, during the four seasons they have been running, have annually carried from 25,000 to 30,000 passengers and have never met with the slightest accident, nor had the enjoyment of a voyage marred by a disturbance on board. Incidentally, also, it might be added that the boat crews have, during the four years, saved twenty-two lives of persons who have accidentally got into the lake while boating in small crafts and thus the line of steamers affords some insurance against death to those who go boating on Quinsigamond.[3]

Part of this last statement was true--the history of this period is replete with accounts of a multitude of boating and swimming mishaps. Some people who went canoeing, rowing, or sailing had absolutely no idea how to operate their particular craft, and the steamboats were instrumental in helping these unfortunates.

However, in stark contrast to the idyllic steamboat voyages described in the advertising brochure, the greatest disaster ever to strike the lake was in the offing. During the week of July 4, 1879, the lake was in full swing, building up to a glorious Fourth of July celebration. The Full Moon Trotting Park in Edgemere had scheduled "FUN FOR THE MILLION!" for July Fourth, consisting of a horse race with a purse of $75, and a match race for $100, with $30 added; three well known horses were racing, and there was a ten mile foot race. Other scheduled activities included a greased pig, a greased pole climbing contest, a tub race, and a sack race.[4]

The steam yacht *Parole*, which could accommodate twenty peo-

[1] Edward R. Fiske, *Pleasure Resorts in Worcester County*, Worcester, MA, 1877.

[2] Polly Lindi, "When Venus Was Queen of the Lake," *Worcester Sunday Telegram*, August 25, 1968.

[3] Fiske.

[4] Advertisement, *Worcester Evening Gazette*, July 3, 1879.

Boating on Lake Quinsigamond (photo, Picturesque Worcester, 1895)

ple comfortably, was available for trips on the northern half of the lake, or "above the causeway" as it was then called. The boat could be chartered for afternoon or evening trips at $2.50 for the first hour, $1.50 for the second hour and $1.00 for each additional hour. The public was notified by a placard at Union Station in Washington Square when it was to be so engaged.[5] Of course, a variety of amusements including fireworks and band concerts were offered to celebrate Independence Day in true American fashion.

In addition, a new steamer had recently been placed in operation on the lake by Jesse Johnson Coburn's boat company. The New Palace Steamer *Col. Isaac Davis* had started regular trips on Wednesday, June 25, 1879. A newspaper ad of the day states, "The boat is entirely New, is a Double Decker, and will carry 300 passengers."[6] When an acquaintance ran into J. J. Coburn at the Lake House on the Fourth, he asked him, "How is your boat getting along?" and Coburn answered, "Pretty well, [I] think I will give Harthan a sweat."[7]

Of course, the great crowds of people that came by carriage, on the Dummy Railroad and on foot to Lincoln Park on the Fourth were anxious to take a trip on the new steamer. The *Col. Isaac Davis* began running at six o'clock in the morning. At quarter past two in the afternoon, the steamer was just completing its seventh round trip and heading for the wharf. It was at this point that what had begun as an idyllic summer holiday, full of fun and excitement, quickly turned into a horrific nightmare.[8]

The crowd at the landing, estimated at 1,000 people, surged towards the steamer in what was later described as "that swinish instinct which too often seizes upon crowds--to push its way anywhere without regard to consequences."[9] The steamer had barely docked when the crowd, despite frantic efforts by J. J. Coburn and Jesse Barker to keep them back, swarmed aboard before the roughly 200 passengers already waiting to disembark could do so.[10]

As the crowd pushed and shoved to get aboard, many rushed to the upper, or "hurricane," deck. The sudden shift in weight threw the boat off balance. It tilted over, away from the wharf, throwing the passengers towards the rail. Several were thrown off the deck and into the water, estimated to be ten feet deep at this particular place. This in turn caused the boat to roll over even more severely.[11]

At this point, the hull became stuck on part of the dock, sealing the boat's fate. The great weight of the passengers was too much; the inadequate wooden stanchions, or supports, holding the upper deck collapsed. The results were catastrophic--the entire upper deck came crashing down, passengers and all, onto the hull and into the water, and on top of those struggling to swim to shore. The safety valve on the steam boiler was destroyed, creating a huge roar as the steam escaped, which only added to the horror and chaos.[12]

People swam for shore or the nearby wharf; some grabbed onto the destroyed hulk of the steamboat, others clung to part of the roof that was by now floating off into the lake. People on shore rushed to the aid of the victims, and soon injured people were everywhere.[13] Immediately a force of twenty police officers was dispatched to the scene, met by his honor, Mayor Pratt, who took charge of the rescue operations along

[5] Ibid.

[6] Ibid.

[7] *Worcester Daily Telegram*, Court Calendar, February 8, 1881.

[8] "Terrible Disaster," *Worcester Evening Gazette*, July 5, 1879.

[9] Quote from the *New York Tribune*, July 5, 1879 found in the *Worcester Evening Gazette*, July 7, 1879.

[10] "Yesterday's Disaster," *Worcester Evening Gazette*, July 5, 1879.

[11] Ibid.

[12] Ibid.

[13] Ibid.

"The pleasure of the voyage is well attested by the fact that the boats, during the four seasons they have been running, have annually carried from 25,000 to 30,000 passengers...." --Pleasure Resorts in Worcester County, 1877 (photo, Picturesque Worcester, 1895)

with Mrs. Pratt, who "rendered much valuable aid." A group of doctors also rushed to help the wounded--a *Worcester Evening Gazette* reporter states that no less than ten were "noticed" at the scene.[14]

The first rumor to reach the city was that the boiler on the steamer *Addie* had exploded, an event greatly feared by steamboat operators of that era, with thirty people supposedly killed and fifty wounded.[15] The wreck, as described in the *Worcester Evening Gazette*, "[had] the appearance of the first rumor, 'an explosion'": the hull of the boat lay off the shore and clear to the water's edge; the engine and machinery were broken; and the smokestack and part of the upper deck were floating halfway across the lake. Other parts of the boat had floated to the eastern shore of the lake.[16]

People rushed to the scene of the disaster, inquiring after friends or relatives that might have been on board. It was widely believed that there were many more people drowned than had been found by nightfall. By the next day, it turned out that the number killed was far less than originally rumored, five to be exact. One other person, Thomas Burns, drowned in an unrelated incident while bathing at the lake. The list of those killed included:[17]

A Mr. Cahill, reported as "John" or "Patrick," died. He and his two daughters were among the dead. His daughter Lizzie was pulled out of the water within "five or eight minutes" after the accident grappled with a boat hook, already dead. Mr. Cahill was pulled out shortly after, with a wound on the back of his head, "apparently dead." The other child's body was not found until later that day.

Lewis Lachapelle was another casualty. He had "$40 in money and a Savings Bank book for $100 on his person," the Worcester Evening Gazette reported. Later it was learned that just before the accident, he was asked by a friend what he should do in the event of a wreck, since he could not swim. He replied, "I should go to the bottom."[18] No sooner had he spoken these words than the disaster occurred and he did, indeed, do just as he had said.

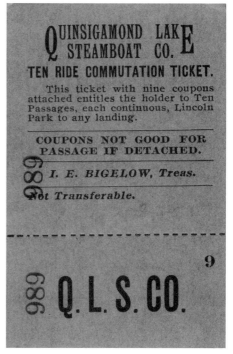

Above: Lake Quinsigamond Steamboat Company tickets, circa 1900 (author's collection)

[14] Ibid.
[15] Ibid.
[16] Ibid.
[17] Ibid.
[18] "The Lake Disaster," Local Matters, *Worcester Evening Gazette*, July 7, 1879.

*On the steamer boat landing at Lincoln Park
(photo, Picturesque Worcester, 1895)*

Miss Maggie Sugrue, first reported as "Nellie Shuckrow," also died. She and her sister were passengers on the trip just completed. She lived at No. 12 Bridge Street in Worcester, and was reported to have been "a very worthy and beautiful girl."[19] A rumor circulated after the wreck that she was the "same girl so seriously wounded by a razor in the hands of a colored man in Mechanic Street" a year or so earlier, but this was dispelled with the observation that "inasmuch as that girl's name was Courtney, the story is incorrect."[20]

Of course, many people were injured, some slightly, others more seriously. Prominent among these were members of the French Band, which had just boarded the steamer on their way to an engagement at the Full Moon Trotting Park in Edgemere. Some of the band members were on the upper deck when the wreck occurred, others were on the lower deck. Most escaped with fairly minor injuries, but their instruments, uniforms, and music were mostly destroyed.[21] Nevertheless, these musicians rescued at least three ladies. One, Hiram Sorrell, saved a woman though she "fastened herself upon him with the proverbial 'drowning clutch.'"[22]

Even after the disaster there were problems. One man berated the crowd with "a storm of reproaches" after he and his two young daughters had been rescued from the wreck, because his children had lost their Sunday hats.[23] Before the throngs of people in the area knew exactly what had happened, many who had purchased tickets rushed to the ticket office near the wharf, causing "something like a riot." They made "loud and angry demands for the refunding of money" before the police restored order. Shortly after, when they learned the full extent of what had happened, the hubbub subsided.[24]

As though things weren't bad enough, the same day a furious storm, described as a tornado, swept through the lake area. Commander Harthan had his steamboat moored to the wharf at the Eyrie Hotel. When he saw the storm approaching he ran to the boat, but he didn't have time to set sail before the storm struck. It ripped the wharf off its foundation and pushed the steamboat out into the lake. When the squall subsided, the boat, with the wharf in tow, made its way back to shore without further incident.[25]

One additional event occurred before the day ended, "illustrating the frightened condition of the parties who were involved in the accident." A young couple, described as "a Scotchman and his lassie," were making their way back to the city in the driving rainstorm. The woman had been thrown overboard in the wreck and was rescued, although she had lost her hat and the "waist" of her dress had been torn off. They made it almost to the intersection of Main and Front Streets before the woman realized her condition, stopping and screaming, "Good Heavens, Jamie, what shall I do! I've no clothes on!" The newspaper reported, "It was her first knowledge that she was not dressed for a street promenade."[26]

All in all, July 4, 1879 had not been a very good day at the lake, but by July 7, the steamboats *Addie* and *Parole* were once again booming with business; the *Parole* ventured through the opening in the causeway to sail on the north end of the lake. Business was so good that the crowds at Quinsigamond Park were "sufficiently numerous to devour all the clams which Dan Moulton baked for them."[27]

---

[19] "Yesterday's Disaster," *Worcester Evening Gazette*, July 5, 1879.

[20] "The Lake Disaster," Local Matters, *Worcester Evening Gazette*, July 7, 1879.

[21] "Yesterday's Disaster," *Worcester Evening Gazette*, July 5, 1879.

[22] Ibid.

[23] "The Lake Disaster," Local Matters, *Worcester Evening Gazette*, July 7, 1879.

[24] Ibid.

[25] "Yesterday's Disaster," *Worcester Evening Gazette*, July 5, 1879.

[26] "The Lake Disaster," Local Matters, *Worcester Evening Gazette*, July 7, 1879.

[27] Ibid.

Worcester, Mass.. Lake Quinsigamond, Lincoln Park, View at Steamboat Landing.

(Postcard, author's collection.)

The *Col. Isaac Davis* steamboat incident was editorialized not only in the local papers, but as far away as New York and Providence. The fact that another accident involving a steamboat had occurred in Trenton, New Jersey only heightened interest in the affair: a crowd rushing to board a steamer there was so large that the wharf collapsed from the weight, resulting in a number of casualties.[28]

The *New York Herald* called for "stern dealings" with whomever was determined at fault so that they "may have the effect to prevent such terrible scenes hereafter." The *Worcester Evening Gazette* likewise reflected that "the only rule for corporations running public conveyances is to take every safeguard to protect the public and not trust at all to their sense of caution. A crowd does not stop to weigh chances or discuss probabilities. They only push on, without much thought of any kind, and nothing more can reasonably be expected of them. Under the circumstances, it is perhaps remarkable that no more lives were lost."[29]

Just what were the circumstances that caused this disaster? An investigation began immediately. Many "experts" in a number of fields were asked to view the wrecked hulk of the *Col. Isaac Davis*. They ranged from architects to carpenters to district attorneys and so on.[30]

A visitor to the city, Capt. G. H. Wyatt of Toronto, Canada, who was employed by the Collingwood and Lake Superior Line and was a "Dominion Inspector of Hulls," inspected the wreck. He declared the hull and power plant well built, noting that special attention had been paid to the boilers.[31]

All of the inspections and testimonies pointed to one undeniable fact: the upper "hurricane" deck on the *Col. Isaac Davis* could not support a large amount of weight because the deck supports were all wooden--no metal supports or braces were used. Thus with the sudden influx of 350 passengers, the supports "snapped like pipe stems."[32]

Ironically, when the boat was being built, the builders wrote to the US Inspector of steamboats in Boston, MA at the request of Mr. Coburn. They asked for an official to come inspect the vessel, but the request was declined because the lake was considered a "State water" and not within the jurisdiction of the United States' steamboat laws.[33]

After conducting an extensive investigation and several interviews with eyewitnesses and survivors, a number of conclusions were reached. It was discovered that the boat was not licensed to operate. Although J. J. Coburn had properly licensed his boat with the appropriate authorities on June 28, the fact that he then sold the boat to his brother, J. C. Coburn, on the same day, made the license invalid. The Coburns had applied to have the license transferred, but the City Clerk declined to do so until the petition could go before the Alderman, which had not happened by the time of the accident.[34] In addition, although Coburn had applied to have the boat licensed to carry 350 passengers, the City Engineer, Mr. Allen, issued a license to carry only 175 people.[35] This was contrary to the newspaper advertisement which stated that the boat would begin regular trips on June 25 with a capacity of 300.[36]

One year after the steamboat incident, on the Fourth of July

[28] Quote from the *New York Herald*, July 5, 1879 found in "The Lake Disaster," Local Matters, *Worcester Evening Gazette*, July 7, 1879.

[29] "The Lake Disaster," Local Matters, *Worcester Evening Gazette*, July 7, 1879.

[30] Ibid.

[31] "Yesterday's Disaster," **Worcester Evening Gazette**, July 5, 1879.

[32] "The Lake Disaster," Local Matters, *Worcester Evening Gazette*, July 7, 1879.

[33] Ibid.

[34] "Yesterday's Disaster," *Worcester Evening Gazette*, July 5, 1879.

[35] Ibid.

[36] Advertisement, *Worcester Evening Gazette*, July 3, 1879.

*Launching the steamboat Uncle Sam at Lake Quinsigamond
(photo courtesy of J. Ronald Bigelow)*

1880, great precautions were taken to prevent another disaster. The repaired *Col. Isaac Davis* had been renamed the *City of Worcester* and was in service on the lake. Unlike the previous year, "every precaution was taken against accident: a detail of officers kept the crowd under control and the passengers were admitted by ticket; as soon as the number allowed by the license board (125) was on board, the gate was closed and the boat started."[37] In a 1937 interview, eighty-five-year-old Edgar Goodwill, a crew member on the *City of Worcester,* remembered that it took some time before people felt comfortable riding on this steamboat.[38]

All that remained from the previous year was the undeniable fact that five people had died on July 4, 1879. Judge Hartley Williams made his report: "Indictments have been found against J. J. Coburn and J. C. Coburn, for causing the death of persons at the lake disaster July 4, 1879. They are in two counts and are brought under the same statute as indictments against Railroad Corporations, where deaths are caused by negligence or carelessness."[39] They were promptly brought to court, where they were arraigned, pleaded not guilty, and released on $5,000 bail each, and their lawyer, Col. Isaac Bullock, was unavailable to represent them. A one week continuance was granted, and then another, until the case was turned over to the Superior Court and delayed until October.[40]

The trial dragged on and on. By January 1880 the defense requested another continuance, "on the grounds that J. J. Coburn for many years has not been able to endure the rigors of the northern winters; he had been south for ten or twelve years and was at present in Florida by advice of a physician."[41] The prosecution objected to the delay, but the trial was again postponed until November 1880.[42]

It was not until February 1881 that the trial really began, in spite of one last ditch effort by Col. Bullock to obtain another continuance. His attempt to gain more time was based on an amazing charge--he claimed that none other than H. H. Bigelow, because of disagreements with J. J. Coburn over the control of the "Dummy" railroad, was the force behind the case to prosecute Coburn. Further, he contended that Bigelow was "rendering pecuniary assistance" to the prosecution "for the purpose of harassing the defendants, and especially Mr. J. J. Coburn."[43]

But the court was not in a mood to be trifled with. This case had been postponed for over eighteen months since the disaster, and apparently this was long enough for the judge. He point blank asked the prosecution counsel if they were in any way connected to Mr. Bigelow, and they both replied in the negative, so the case proceeded.[44]

After two weeks of extensive testimony by witness after witness, the jury declared J. J. Coburn guilty of manslaughter in the death of Patrick Cahill. His brother J. C. Coburn was found not guilty.[45] The residents of the Lake View section of the city held a series of meetings in support of Coburn, calling for a new trial. Their efforts were in vain.[46]

The disaster and resulting trial proved such a shock to J. J. Coburn that he never fully recovered. In 1883 he turned over his boat rental

37 "At the Lake," *Worcester Evening Gazette,* July 6, 1880.

38 "Lake Quinsigamond has gone 'Sissy,' says Steamboater of Fifty Years Ago," *Worcester Sunday Telegram,* January 10, 1937.

39 Court Calendar, *Worcester Evening Gazette,* October 27, 1879.

40 "The Recent Disaster," *Worcester Evening Gazette,* August 1, 1879.

41 Court Calendar, *Worcester Evening Gazette,* January 28, 1880.

42 Ibid.

43 Court Calendar, *Worcester Evening Gazette,* February 7, 1881.

44 Ibid.

45 Court Calendar, *Worcester Evening Gazette,* February 18, 1881.

46 "The Lake View Protest," *Worcester Evening Gazette,* February 18, 1881.

Worcester, Mass., Lake Quinsigamond,
Lincoln Park, Boat Landing.

The steamboat landing is at the south-east corner of Quinsigamond Grove, or Lincoln Park, as it is now more commonly called. Here a cute little wharf has been erected, with pleasant seats under the shade of neighboring trees; and from this point at every hour during the pleasant summer days and moonlight nights the captain's "all aboard" announces the "clearing" of the steamboats. (postcard, author's collection)

20

business to his son, A. A. Coburn (Alvarado Alonzo, for whom Alvarado Avenue is named), and sold the rest of his lake holdings, citing his failing health as the reason.[47] Despite whatever past problems they might have had, his remaining lake property was sold to Horace H. Bigelow. Still in poor health, Coburn, a broken man who was described as "genial, generous, popular; fond of good fellowship," died in 1886 at the age of 53.[48] He would only live long enough to fulfill part of his dream of developing the shores of the lake into a huge tourist area. What might have been, even with the reported rivalry between J. J. Coburn and H. H. Bigelow, had the disaster never occurred? The lake might have become an even greater amusement center than it eventually was.

The steamboats were a source of great pleasure to thousands of people through the years. What happened to these pleasure boats that leisurely transported passengers up and down the lake, "tootling" to others along the way?

The steamboat *Apollo*, after almost twenty years of cruising on the lake, was taken out of service after the 1903 season. When the finishing touches were being added to the new White City amusement park in April 1905, the boat was sold by Irving E. Bigelow, son of H. H. Bigelow, to an unnamed buyer.[49] The new owner planned to give the old steamboat a fresh coat of paint and place it on the midway at White City. The younger Bigelow was happy to hear of this plan to preserve the steamer, since the *Apollo* had a long history at the lake; it was used as the referee's boat in many of the famous regattas held there over the years.[50]

Unfortunately, the workmen trying to finish the boardwalk area at White City didn't appreciate the boat's historic background. They wanted to get it out of the way so they could finish their job, and they advised Irving Bigelow to break the old boat up for junk. Bigelow didn't agree.[51] Not long after, his father H. H. Bigelow was visiting the park. He didn't know the boat had been sold and the workmen convinced him to let them destroy it. Thus the *Apollo* was "taken apart more quickly than if dashed upon the rocks in a storm." When the new owner came looking for the boat and learned that it had been destroyed, he was furious, doing "other things beside a war dance," swearing and using foul language.[52]

After a brief investigation, it was discovered that H. H. Bigelow had indeed given the go ahead for the boat's destruction, which he greatly regretted upon learning the real story. This was a particularly tragic end for the steamer, considering that the Bigelows had been approached by two men who wanted to recreate what was known as the "Gen. Slocum disaster" that had occurred in New York.[53] Their plan was to fill the hapless *Apollo* with human dummies and set it ablaze. Bigelow rejected their idea, earning the praise of newspapers from here to New York for his efforts to preserve the old steamboat. Neither "war dancing," swearing, nor regret could in any way bring the poor *Apollo* back. Thus part of the lake's history was lost forever. [54]

The remains of a steamboat were found in 1960 by "frogmen" diving at Lincoln Park near where the *Col. Isaac Davis* accident had taken place. At the time, it was speculated that this must be the *Col. Isaac Davis/City of Worcester,* but it could have been any one of a

[47] Charles Nutt, A. B., *History of Worcester and Its People*, New York: Lewis Historical Publishing Co., 1919, pp. 750-751.
[48] Ibid.
[49] *Worcester Daily Telegram*, April 15, 1905.
[50] Ibid.
[51] Ibid.
[52] Ibid.
[53] Ibid.
[54] Ibid.

number of steamboats. No positive identification was ever made.[55] However, the discovery of the remains of this steamboat did bring forward someone who witnessed the *Col. Isaac Davis* disaster, Edgar W. Norton of Norton Way in Shrewsbury. Norton, who lived in an old log cabin for sixty-odd years, was eight years old when the wreck occurred. Along with his brother Frank and father Jabez, he had gone to Lincoln Park on that fateful Fourth of July seeking relief from the heat. They were only a few yards away when the disaster happened. Davis' father forced his way through the crowd to rescue two people struggling in the water.[56]

However unfortunate, it is most likely that many of these steamboats, these "miniature things of beauty" which had provided pleasure for so many people, simply fell into disuse and were left to rot away at their moorings.

[55] Tony Mastro, "Frogmen Find Capsized Steamer," *Worcester Daily Telegram*, August 19, 1959.

[56] Al Bartkevious, "Shrewsbury Recalls Isaac Davis Disaster," *Worcester Daily Telegram*, August 20, 1959.

COLLEGE REGATTA—BOAT-RACE BETWEEN THE YALE AND HARVARD BOYS ON LAKE QUINSIGAMOND, JULY 28, 1865.

Starting in 1857, boat races, or regattas, were held at Lake Quinsigamond.... The biggest college rivalry was between Harvard and Yale, and Harvard predominated, winning seven of their first nine contests. (from Harper's Weekly, 1865)

BOAT CLUBS AND REGATTAS

Before 1860, the area surrounding Lake Quinsigamond was a pristine wilderness. With the exceptions of a floating bridge at the site of the current Route 9 bridge and the Pond Tavern House located north of the bridge on the Shrewsbury shore, there was very little development in this area.

QUINSIGAMOND BOAT CLUB (QBC)

It was only when boat clubs were organized on the lake that people began to take more of an interest in the area. The first of these was the Quinsigamond Boat Club (QBC), which was formed by a small group of men who met "first for a row at the Pond" in October 1857.[1] At this time there were only four boats on the lake: a whale boat with a sail and long oars, two rowboats, and Dr. John Green's lifeboat ("made of sheet iron but unsinkable"), which was also the first boat used by the Quinsigamond club.[2]

This club was soon followed by the "Wide Awake Club," which rowed at Salisbury Pond, and the "Atalanta Boat Club" in 1859. The Atalanta Boat Club first rowed at Curtis Pond but relocated at Lake Quinsigamond with its boat, the "Phantom." This boat was purchased by the Quinsigamonds, who built a boathouse with the Atalantas on the Shrewsbury side of the lake, just south of the present bridge. The boathouse was moved to the Worcester shore in 1862, standing at

what would later be the site of the Coburn boathouse. In 1864 a shell was purchased by the club and named the "Quinsigamond." In June 1875, a clubhouse was erected near Regatta Point and the group became a formal organization. The QBC continued to grow, and in 1883 it built a new clubhouse that later included a fine restaurant and tennis courts.[3]

Starting in 1857, boat races, or regattas, were held at the lake, and the Quinsigamonds did very well in the standings. The club promoted the college regattas on the lake and offered the hospitality of their club after the races finished. The biggest college rivalry was between Harvard and Yale, and Harvard predominated, winning seven of their first nine contests. In addition, Brown, Amherst, Cornell, and other colleges rowed at the lake during these early years. As time passed, the club became more involved in presenting plays and musicals at local theaters, and less involved with rowing activities. Eventually the ages of the members increased and the club became strictly a social organization, presumably still "exclusive in its membership."[4]

The Quinsigamond Boat Club disbanded in 1948. The clubhouse itself, located on Lake Avenue, then became the Italian American or ITAM club. In 1953 the building, like so much of the lake's history, went up in flames and was destroyed; the more modern

---

[1] *The Quinsigamond Boat Club of Worcester, Massachusetts, 1857-1917*, Quinsigamond Boat Club, Worcester, Mass., 1917, p. 5.

[2] Ibid.

[3] *The Quinsigamond Boat Club of Worcester, Massachusetts, 1857-1917*, pp. 5-10. Also see Charles Nutt, A. B., *History of Worcester and Its People*, New York: Lewis Historical Publishing Co., 1919, p. 965.

[4] *Picturesque Views on and Adjacent to the Routes of the Worcester Consolidated Street Railway and at Lake Quinsigamond*, Worcester, Mass.: The Worcester Consolidated Street Railway Company, 1898, p. 93. Also see Franklin P. Rice, *Dictionary of Worcester (Massachusetts) and its Vicinity*, Worcester, Mass.: F. S. Blanchard & Co., 1889, p. 15.

The Quinsigamond Boat Club's (QBC) clubhouse
When boat clubs were organized at Lake Quinsigamond, people began
to take more of an interest in the area. The first boat club, the QBC,
was founded in 1857. (photo reprinted with permission from the
Worcester Public Library, circa 1898)

ITAM club building later took its place. Today even the ITAM club is defunct, the building's future uncertain.

A modern-day successor to the QBC was formed by a group of local boating enthusiasts in the 1980s. Although not as formally organized as its predecessor, the group issues yearly commemorative momentoes bearing the distinctive QBC logo and holds periodic gatherings.

LAKESIDE BOAT CLUB · · · · · · · · · · · · · · · · · · ·

The Lakeside Boat Club was organized on February 14, 1887 and was incorporated the same year. The club members worked as clerks in the city's offices and banks and the group was very active in promoting rowing activities on the lake.[5] The clubhouse itself was erected on Lake Avenue, just south of Lincoln Park. The building contained seven large rooms on the first floor and a hall used for banquets or dances on the second. The third floor had rooms for members to sleep in. Boats and canoes were stored in the basement, which had doors opening out onto a dock area.[6] An 1898 description of the club follows: "The Lakeside's club house is near Lincoln Park, and has a large number of handsome boats and canoes, and its members, mostly young men, give numerous pleasant socials and receptions at their handsome quarters."[7] Their clubhouse was later used by the Norton Company as a boathouse and then served as an armory for the Naval Reserve.[8] Their large brown clubhouse still stands at 95 Lake Avenue; it has been an apartment building for many years.

WACHUSETT BOAT CLUB · · · · · · · · · · · · · · · · · · ·

In 1887, its first year of existence, the Wachusett Boat Club occu-

pied the same clubhouse later used by the Lakesides. In 1888, the club moved to the old theater building on Ramshorn Island and stayed there for eleven years before relocating to Shrewsbury. This clubhouse was eventually destroyed by a fire. In 1902, the group moved back to Ramshorn Island and occupied what had been the Belmont House hotel until it disbanded in 1908. Between 1887 and 1908, the club's members compiled an impressive record of accomplishments, not only on the local scene, but at the national and international levels as well.[9] These events set the stage for a great string of rowing accomplishments by the Lake Quinsigamond oarsmen.

In 1889, Fred Haas won the junior scullers race with Thomas Higgins, who also won the intermediate and senior sculling races. The club entered Worcester's first eight-oared crew in the National Regatta in 1890 at Lake Quinsigamond. Largely through the club's efforts, this race was also held at Lake Quinsigamond in 1902, 1903, and 1906.[10] The club set the record for intermediate eight crew at Saratoga Lake in New York in 1895. That same year, club members Edward Hanlan and "Ned" Ten Eyck won the junior class race; they also won the intermediate race at Saratoga in 1896.[11]

In 1897, "Ned" Ten Eyck, wearing the blue and white colors of the Wachusett Boat Club, won the Diamond Sculls at the Royal Henley Regatta in England. The *Worcester Evening Post* recalled this event a number of years later: "In that classic event, to which the oarsmen of the world aspire, this 18-year-old Worcester boy gave backwash to the field and electrified the world by his remarkable victory. It was the first time an American had ever won the Henley fix-

[5] Rice, p. 16.

[6] Nutt, p. 966.

[7] *Picturesque Views on and Adjacent to the Routes of the Worcester Consolidated Street Railway and at Lake Quinsigamond*, pp. 93-97.

[8] *Worcester Evening Post*, July 10, 1926.

[9] Nutt, p. 967.

[10] Ibid.

[11] Ibid.

In May 1900 the YMCA boathouse had just opened for the season with new shrubs, trees and flower beds, in addition to a new selection of magazines available in the living room and a piano in the social room.
(postcard, author's collection, circa 1900)

ture."[12] Upon his return from England, Ten Eyck was given a hero's welcome. The lake residents came to the celebration en masse because he was one of them. From the time of his Diamond Sculls victory, Ten Eyck won every American championship single and every American championship double (with Charles Lewis) until he retired in 1902.[13] In 1900, the Wachusett Four, Ten Eyck, Charles Lewis, Cornelius Daly, and Thomas Johnson, won the International Four in New York.

Ten Eyck's father was the well known "Old" Jim Ten Eyck, who was the rowing coach at Syracuse from 1905 to 1938. The elder Ten Eyck had also been closely associated with many of the "old school" scullers at the Lake, including George H. Hosmer, George Bubear, George Plaisted, John Teemer, Jake Gaudaur, and Edward Hanlan, who set a world's professional record for the three mile race at Lake Quinsigamond in 1886 (19 minutes, 23 seconds), and for whom "Old" Jim Ten Eyck's son was named.[14]

OTHER CLUBS ·

In May 1900 an article in the *Worcester Telegram* described the YMCA boathouse, which had just opened for the season with new shrubs, trees, and flower beds, in addition to a new selection of magazines available in the reading room and a piano in the social room. Two new and larger canoes had been added to the group's fleet, which numbered over thirty. New games included a double shuffleboard and a half-size board located in the boys' room. The club sported a new dock that year, along with a swimming wharf complete with a "strong spring board" for diving and a diving tower. The boathouse, in accordance with the rules of the YMCA, was closed on Sundays, although religious meetings were held at the group's winter quarters in the city each Sunday afternoon.[15]

Other boat clubs soon followed. These included the Worcester Boat Club, which was later home to the Crescents and still later to the Kalumets, a boat club run by the YMCA, and the aforementioned Norton Company boat club.[16] During the 1902 season the Quincy Boat Club occupied what had been the Lake View House hotel, and quickly settled into the lake's crew racing scene.[17]

CREW RACING ·

Starting in 1895 Edward J. Kerns, Sr. began coaching a crew of high school boys from Worcester. This crew became the first schoolboy eight in the country. They won the intermediate class in the national regatta held at Philadelphia in 1896, where they were sent by public subscriptions.[18] The same year they raced the Wachusett Boat Club team. The *Worcester Post* reminisced about the outcome in a 1926 article:

And that same year, how the old dope was upset when those same schoolboys defeated the crack Wachusett eight in a special race at the lake. That Wachusett crew, perhaps the best that ever rowed for that great club, the previous year had established a world record for 1 1/2 miles at Saratoga, 7.33 1/2, which mark still holds. If the high school crew's win at Philadelphia had thrilled the aquatic world, its victory over the Wachusett eight enriched many a backer as the bettors figured the race easy for the club crew. Much money changed hands on that race in which 16-17 year old boys set the railbirds gasping. It was as hectic a race as the historic old course has ever seen.

12 *Worcester Evening Post*, July 10, 1926.

13 Nutt, p. 967.

14 *Worcester Evening Post*, July 10, 1926.

15 "Lake Season Stirs Interest," *Worcester Daily Telegram*, May 2, 1900.

16 *Worcester Evening Post*, July 10, 1926.

17 *Worcester Daily Telegram*, May 5, 1902.

18 Ibid.

Champion oarsmen rowing on Lake Quinsigamond
(photo, Picturesque Worcester, 1895)

Though crew racing activities dwindled at Lake Quinsigamond for a few years, 1937 saw a rebirth of great crew events. This was largely due to the efforts of one man, Kenneth F. Burns, who was a Shrewsbury police officer at the time (later he became chief of the department). Burns was an accomplished sculler in his own right, one of the fastest in New England; he won every race he entered from 1922 to 1925. In 1925, he and Fred Haas won the Senior Double Sculls event and set a new lake record with a time of 9 minutes, 13 seconds.[19]

His first goal was to start a rowing team at Shrewsbury High School, which he accomplished despite a lack of financial assistance and a lack of racing shells. The Shrewsbury boys learned the sport using planks as make-believe boats instead of real racing shells. Through Burns' efforts, local businessmen and sportsmen were enlisted to support the fledgling program. These men included Ed Cunningham of the New England Rowing Association, Works Progress Administration (WPA) crew coach Sam Wright, Shrewsbury businessman and sports enthusiast T. Frank Hickey, and Chester Condon. A Boston businessman and rowing enthusiast, W. Bruce Pirney, donated equipment to the club.[20] Coach Burns also convinced some Ivy League colleges to contribute racing shells that they no longer used. Soon they had two old eight-oared shells and a set of oars.[21] One of the shells, contributed by Yale University, was known as the "Dipsy Doodle" because it was so warped, according to Mrs. Barbara (Burns) Caron of Shrewsbury, Coach Burns' daughter.

After only six weeks of instruction, conducted at all hours to fit around Coach Burns' shifts at the police department, the novice crew won the first race they entered. They defeated the more experienced Worcester North High School, winning by six lengths. Granted, the North High boat had an oar break at the 3/4 mile mark, but the Shrewsbury boat was already ahead by three lengths at that point. Since the course was only one mile long, the Shrewsbury boat most certainly would have won either way.[22]

This victory was followed by a journey to the 54th Annual Regatta of the New England Amateur Rowing Association held at the Charles River Basin. The local boys faced crews from the Union Boat Club of Boston and the Shawmut Boat Club of South Boston, both of which were long-established groups.[23] Coach Burns had confidence that his rowers would make a good showing despite their inexperience. He was quoted in the local paper: "They're a fine lot, faithful and honest in their effort. We cannot more than hope for victory against crews which the Unions and Shawmuts rate highly enough to enter a New England regatta, but the boys are game and they will make it a battle anyway."[24] The coach need not have worried: his team won a stunning upset victory. The two veteran crews were defeated and the Shrewsbury crew went on to bigger and better things.

Finally, they went to the National Regatta in Buffalo, New York.[25] Their opponents, the Lafayette High School crew from Buffalo, were in their hometown. In a finish described as "tissue close," the judges first declared Shrewsbury the winner, only to reverse their decision a few moments later, awarding the race to the Lafayette crew! They claimed that the Lafayette boat won by one-fifth of a second.[26] The crestfallen young men from Shrewsbury returned to a grand welcome, despite their loss. A crowd estimated at 2,000 people, including the

---

[19] Fred J. Harvey, "A Tribute to Kenneth F. Burns - Mr. Rowing of 1952," undated.

[20] *Worcester Sunday Telegram*, June 2, 1940.

[21] Ibid.

[22] Undated newspaper clipping, courtesy of Mrs. Barbara Caron.

[23] Undated newspaper clipping, courtesy of Mrs. Barbara Caron.

[24] Ibid.

[25] Undated newspaper clipping, courtesy of Mrs. Barbara Caron.

[26] Harvey.

From The Lake Quinsigamond Boat Club 1857 - 1917, author's collection.

Mayor of Worcester, greeted them at Union Station. They were parad-
ed through downtown Worcester in a motorcade before moving on to
Shrewsbury, where they were greeted by bands, singing and red flares.
Official ceremonies were held on the Shrewsbury Common, where a
reception committee sang the praises of the Shrewsbury oarsmen.[27]
Then Coach Burns himself came forward, speaking glowingly of his
team and their outstanding performance. He was convinced that they
were, at the very least, entitled to a draw in the race, but he had decided that no protest would be filed. There would be other races and
other crews to beat.[28]

In 1939 they faced their old Lafayette rivals once more, this time
in the Junior Schoolboy Championship in Boston. They competed
with a very accomplished crew from Philadelphia's St. Thomas More
Academy. Most people didn't give the Shrewsbury crew a chance.[29]
The Shrewsbury crew proved them wrong, however. By the halfway
point, Lafayette was clearly behind, with Shrewsbury and St. Thomas
More fighting it out for the lead. Despite a valiant effort by the St.
Thomas More boys, Shrewsbury beat them. The Shrewsbury High
crew, with only three years' experience, had won the National Junior
Schoolboy Championship![30] This was the beginning of a long tradi-
tion of superlatives for Coach Burns and the Shrewsbury High School
crew. Eventually the crew built their own boathouse out of a portable
schoolhouse donated by the town of Shrewsbury and metal roofing
donated by a Worcester boat club.[31] The boathouse was torn down in
July 1997 and this land will become a town park. Shrewsbury High
School now uses Donahue Rowing Center for a boathouse.

Coach Burns was instrumental in bringing many rowing activities
to the lake: the Middle States Regatta in 1950, the National Regatta

in 1951, the Olympic trials in 1952, and the Eastern Sprints later on.
To this day, the lake is home to a myriad of rowing activities. The
New England Interscholastic Rowing Association schoolboy races, the
Quinsigamond Cup for local high school crews, the Worcester City
Cup for local colleges, and the Eastern Sprints, among various others,
all use Lake Quinsigamond as their course. Although Burns was the
primary force in promoting crew racing events at the lake, there were
other people who helped, including Kenneth Trinder and Burns' old
racing partner, Fred Haas.

Another person who played a key role in crew events at the lake
was Joseph Garofalo. Starting about 1938, Garofalo began building
crew racing shells and oars at Williams Boat Works on the lake. The
best part of this job, which he says he enjoyed so much he would have
worked for free, was "swimming for free and using the boats for free!"
Garofalo became one of the most popular and respected builders of
crew racing shells. He has been building shells for almost sixty years
and, when asked, he claims to be retired. This may or may not be
true, but as he guides a visitor on a tour through his workshops, he
points out a number of shells of many shapes and sizes in various
stages of completion. A true master of his craft, Garofalo has built
shells for customers all over the world.

Over the years, other Shrewsbury crews excelled: the 1945 team
won the four-oared shell race at the American Scholastic Rowing
Championship in Philadelphia. In the spring of 1995, these same
boys, now men in their late 60s, decided to relive their crew racing
days. They embarked on a 1,000 meter jaunt at their old racing
ground at Lake Quinsigamond, using a four-oared Garofalo shell. The
team, consisting of Raymond Harlow, Richard Leonard, Russell Bath,

---

[28] Ibid.

[29] Undated newspaper clipping, courtesy of Mrs. Barbara Caron.

[30] Undated newspaper clipping, courtesy of Mrs. Barbara Caron.

[31] Ibid.

Ned Cunningham, a well known rower on Lake Quinsigamond, was best known for his feat of stepping into his one man shell and balancing an oar for a few moments without falling overboard, before stepping back onto the dock. He was a fixture at any rowing event in the "good old days" at the lake. (photo courtesy of Richard F. Whitney, Founder and President of Whitney Real Estate, and Doris A. Mathieson)

Russell Nordwell, and Robert Doyle, completed this trip quickly, despite the jibes of their wives, who were nonetheless proud of them. This particular team had aspired to enter the 1948 Olympics and trained together after high school graduation, although they were ultimately unsuccessful in their bid.[32]

In the mid-1970s, Burns encouraged his daughter, Barbara (Burns) Caron, a physical education teacher at Shrewsbury High School, to start a girls' crew. Prior to this, crew was entirely a male affair--no girls allowed. His daughter finally consented, and so another chapter in the Burns story began. A few years later, Burns took his granddaughter, Pamela (Caron) Krause, under his wing, teaching her the fine points of coaching. Barbara Caron retired from coaching in 1994 and Pam Krause continues to coach the Shrewsbury boys' crew. Thus the Burns family has played a huge role in the crew racing scene at the lake for over seventy years. Coach Burns passed away in 1982 after sixty years of personal involvement. This family's dedication to crew racing has made an impact on the sport and has made history at Lake Quinsigamond.

---

[32] *Worcester Telegram and Gazette*, May 27, 1995.

The Tatassit Canoe Club, circa 1898
Their boathouse, completed in September 1891, was landscaped with
shrubs and built in a beautiful location on Plum Island with many
views of the lake from its many porches and windows. (reprinted
with permission from the Worcester Public Library)

LAKE QUINSIGAMOND'S BEACHES-- "TAKING THE AIR" AT THE LAKE

Two of Lake Quinsigamond's most popular attractions, and consequently its most enduring, are the Sunset and Tatassit bathing beaches. Although Sunset Beach was in use as a bathing beach before Tatassit Beach, the latter has a longer overall history, so we shall travel there first.

In the winter of 1889, "five tired but enthusiastic young men" returned from a skating trip to North Grafton and decided to form a canoe club on Lake Quinsigamond. Canoes were virtually unknown on the lake at this time. These five men included Dr. E. W. Finney, Fred P. Dean, A. H. Lange, and Irving E. Bigelow, whose family played a large part in the development of the lake area. Bigelow offered the use of his boathouse as a meeting place for what was to become the Tatassit Canoe Club. Officers were elected to positions including Commodore, Vice Commodore, Purser, and Fleet Captain, even though the group had no canoes.[1]

Club membership was limited to twenty-five at first, but as the club's reputation grew, this restriction was lifted and the club prospered. In January 1891 the club held its first annual banquet and voted to join the American Canoe Association. The club commissioned Mr. A. A. Coburn, the well known boat builder, to build a "war canoe" to hold a crew of twelve. However, in his enthusiasm to make the canoe light, the builder failed to make it sturdy enough. Thus on its first voyage it began filling with water. The crew made it back to shore with great difficulty and then returned the canoe to the builder. Rebuilt, the canoe became "one of the sights of the lake" along with its crew, who were known to

dress in white, black, and orange outfits with the club's logo, the Sunflower Totem, decorating their chests.[2]

As the club outgrew its quarters, its members began a search for a more suitable place to meet. In the summer of 1891 they looked at Sugar Loaf Island briefly, but soon decided that Plum Island would be an ideal spot. A pencil sketch of a proposed clubhouse was prepared, funds raised, and the island purchased. Several members camped out on the island shortly after the club bought it.[3] The noted builder, Mr. J. G. Vaudreuil, a boatsman himself, was contracted to build the clubhouse at a cost of $1,600. The house, completed in September 1891, was landscaped with shrubs and built in a beautiful location with sweeping views of the lake from its many porches and windows. An old photo of the original building shows a stained glass window depicting the club's sunflower logo. From 1895 to 1903 three additions were made to the club's quarters on the island.[4]

In 1894 the club began its tradition of annual shows, called "messes." The first was held at the Belmont Hotel on November 5 of that year. At this time minstrel shows and vaudeville were the rage and the Tatassits were no exception; these productions became quite grand affairs. Old photos show them in full costume, as clowns, Chinamen, sailors, or even in drag, making not so attractive "Tatassit Girls" of the all-male membership. One production concluded with an Amazonian march in which the seven "Amazons," now clean shaven of course, had appeared a few moments before with their beautiful mustaches still intact.[5] The sets for their plays were no less

---

[1] W.J.H. Nourse, Ed., "The Tatassit Totem," pp. 3-4.

[2] Ibid.

[3] Nourse, op cit., pp. 5-6.

[4] Nourse, op cit., p. 7.

[5] Nourse, op cit., pp. 7-21.

In 1894 the Tatassit Canoe Club began its tradition of annual shows, called "messes." These productions became quite grand affairs. (photo from the collections of the Worcester Historical Museum)

elaborate than the costumes. One scene opened with three Tatassits sitting on the handle of a giant pan; another included the famous "Chocomobile," which was propelled around the room by its madcap driver wildly dressed in golfing togs.[6]

The club was also a musical group. One songbook, "War Songs of the Tatassit Canoe Club, Season 1914," contained twenty-one popular selections, including "All Aboard for Dixie Land," "Peg O' My Heart," and "Sit Down! You're Rocking the Boat." A song written by club member Harry W. Doe, "The Totem of the Sun Flower," opened each annual performance:

Chorus
The Totem of the Sunflow'r will drive away the blues
On green Tatassit Island, you do just as you choose.
There's ease, there's sport there's labor
There's quiet or there's fun
That's why I love the Totem of the Flower of the Sun.[7]

By 1928, the canoe club was no longer active, and the lake property was purchased for $15,000 by an ambitious young man named Felix F. Pollet, who was only twenty-eight at the time. While swimming at Sunset Beach, Pollet noticed the large crowds that the beach attracted.[8] Thus he purchased the Tatassit property and quickly developed it into a highly popular lake attraction as the Tatassit Bathing Beach.

Pollet himself was quite an interesting person: by age seventeen he had already owned a tire store; in 1938 he was reportedly the first person to come up with the idea of renting beach chairs on Miami Beach; years later, he was one of the last Americans to leave Cuba after Fidel Castro came to power. A lifelong bachelor, he traveled the world and visited scores of countries when his beach closed for the season.[9]

When Pollet purchased the beach, the site was much more wooded, but eventually it was cleared and a large area of soft, white sand was added. By 1929, Pollet's first season at Tatassit Bathing Beach, he had already added swings, a snack bar, a tower with diving boards, and the "Monster Water Toboggan."[10] A popular attraction, the Monster Water Toboggan was advertised as 60 feet high and 150 feet long. After climbing long flights of stairs, two passengers would sit aboard a heavy wooden sled equipped with wheels that fit into the rails on a roller coaster-like track. They then descended to the water's surface with a thunderous roar, flying along until running out of momentum. Then the sled would sink like a rock and the passengers would swim back to shore with their sled in tow. Although the sleds, or toboggans, were of heavy construction, for many years there was no net or any type of safety device to keep passengers from falling off. This was not usually a problem because most people would hold on for dear life.

This ride was in use well into the 1970s without any notable mishaps occurring. Only after a wire mesh safety net was installed was there a serious accident. A husband and wife decided to try the ride. The problem arose when the wife wanted to get off the ride after starting the downward plunge. Her husband did his best to accommodate her wishes: he stuck out his foot to try to stop the sled. Of course, the wire screen got in the way and he left the better part of his toe behind, not slowing the toboggan in the least. Eventually the Monster Water Toboggan was closed forever, but it certainly lives

---

[6] Nourse, loc cit.

[7] Nourse, op cit., p. 2.

[8] Sibyl Farson, "He's 'Done It All' Says 88-Year-Old," *Worcester Telegram and Gazette*, June 30, 1989.

[9] Obituary of Felix Pollet, *Worcester Telegram and Gazette*, December 24, 1991.

[10] Undated newspaper advertisement, courtesy of Mrs. Judith Godin.

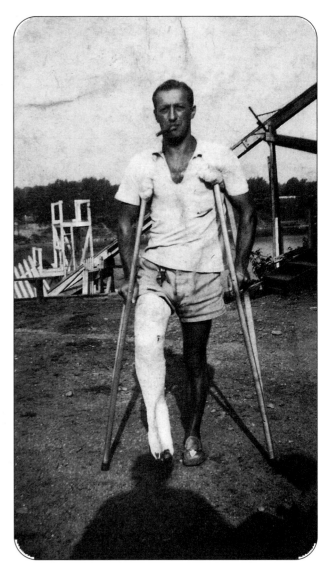

A bird's eye view of Tatassit Beach (above), which was purchased by an ambitious young man, Felix Pollet (right), in 1928. The beach became a popular recreation spot. (both photos courtesy of Judy Godin)

on in the memories of those who were daring enough, or possibly foolish enough, to have ridden it.

One of the most ambitious projects Pollet undertook involved the old Tatassit Canoe Club lodge on Plum Island. When he bought the beach, the lodge was in poor repair and the wooden foot bridge used to reach the island needed work. Two young men, Kenneth Trinder and Joseph Lamotte, made a deal with Pollet to help clean up the building and replace the little bridge in exchange for the use of the lodge hall to hold a dance (Pollet was short of funds and unable to pay them for the work). When the dance was a great success, Pollet decided that Trinder and Lamotte should pay him for the use of the hall because they made so much money. What he didn't realize was that the two men had invited so many of their friends to the dance that they made very little money, and neither did Pollet.

Felix Pollet did, however, transform this clubhouse into a very popular restaurant and nightclub. He managed to retain some remnants of the canoe club days: a newspaper clipping notes, "the Tatassit War Canoe, famous in the annals of Lake Quinsigamond, still roosts majestically in the boathouse of the lodge."[11]

The nightclub, called the Hi-Hat, was decorated in a New York nightlife theme. Today traces of murals that graced the walls can still be seen. It was open during Prohibition, and although Pollet stated in a 1989 newspaper interview that he "just served soft drinks," there are a few people who recall obtaining something a bit stronger at private parties.[12] However, in the days following Prohibition, a full bar was added. The Hi-Hat was very successful and featured a menu with a wide variety of selections.

Pollet continued to improve the beach over time. A bath house

(advertised as having 1,500 lockers), saunas, basketball courts, and a larger snack bar were added. Boats and canoes were available to rent. An "Airial Chute" was installed, with an advertisement reading, "Try our new Airial Chute - It's a Wow!"[13] To try it, one climbed a ladder to a platform, grabbed the T-bar, which was attached to a trolley mechanism, and then stepped off into space, dangling from the bar while the trolley slid down a cable. Most of the time, a trip would end with the rider crash-landing in the water like a duck, although some would drop off mid-trip, tucking into a cannonball and splashing into the lake below.

Problems arose with this ride also. The rope would get tangled in the trolley when pulling the trolley back up to the platform. Once when this happened, a woman slid halfway down the cable and got stuck, with no way to go up or down. After a short time, she let go of the T-bar and fell into the water. Unfortunately, she tensed her legs and shot straight down through the shallow water, striking the bottom and severely fracturing her legs.

Despite the occasional mishap, the beach continued to grow in popularity. Other water attractions included a telephone pole log that rolled madly whenever anyone tried to climb aboard, a barrel configured to look like an elephant, rafts that swimmers could swim out to, and "night swimming." In 1930, one of the first miniature golf courses in the area was installed. Billed as an "obstacle golf course," it was described in the August 9, 1930 edition of the *Leader* newspaper:

Mr. Golfer, want to play that new fangled golf game at a nice, clean, cool and pleasurable retreat? Of course you do. Then hop into the old bus and drive down to Felix Pollet's Tatassit Island Bathing Beach.

---

[11] Undated newspaper clipping, courtesy of Mrs. Judith Godin.

[12] Sibyl Farson, "He's 'Done It All' Says 88-Year-Old," *Worcester Telegram and Gazette*, June 30, 1989.

[13] *Civic Leader*, undated, courtesy of Mrs. Judith Godin.

Felix Pollet transformed the Tatassit Canoe Club's clubhouse on Plum Island into a successful nightclub called the Hi-Hat, which was decorated in a New York nightlife theme. (advertisement, author's collection)

Always with one finger on the trigger of progress, this popular resort has expended many thousands of dollars to install one of the new golf courses for the convenience of its patrons. The game, which is spreading like wildfire throughout the country, is finding a great many adherents in this region. The Tatassit Island course is one of the latest on the market and will afford the players a vast amount of pleasure.

To further insure the pleasure of the patrons, arrangements have been made whereby parents who drive down to the beach with their children can arrange to have the children cared for by attendants while they indulge in the miniature Scotch game.

The beach was such a popular attraction that it was not unusual to have extra busses running on summer weekends. The two parking lots, one on each side of South Quinsigamond Avenue, were filled to overflowing on hot summer days. Photos show crowds of people dotting the sand, swimming in the water, and lined up at the snack bar.

Pollet maintained the beach grounds with meticulous care. Everything was freshly painted each season; and after closing each day, neighborhood children would scour the beach for trash or cigarette butts in return for a small compensation.

During the 1930s, "Miss Tatassit" beauty contests were held at the beach. Contestants, wearing bathing suits and high heels, would walk down a makeshift runway to be judged. Pollet's niece, Judy (Young) Godin, remembers being crowned "Miss Junior Tatassit Beach" every year when she was a little girl. She would receive a beautiful doll as a prize. However, after the contest her uncle would take the doll back and award it to her again when she won the following year!

In 1974, Pollet sold his beloved Tatassit Beach. Because he felt strongly that the town of Shrewsbury needed a place where families could go to relax and enjoy the lake, he first offered to sell the beach to the town. The town declined to purchase it, however, and the beach remained in private hands. Over the ensuing years fewer and fewer people visited the beach. Little by little, sections of the beach were closed due to the drop in attendance. The steam baths were closed in the early 1980s and the summer apartment rentals in the island lodge were discontinued in 1984.

For anyone who remembers the "old days" of crowds packing the beach on hot summer days, a visit to Tatassit today reveals a forlorn shadow of its former glory. The once grand canoe club/nightclub/apartment building on the island is a decaying hulk, with holes in the roof and floors, rotting stairways, and peeling paint. The diving tower, slide, trapeze, and toboggan rides are all gone. The once freshly painted buildings and railings are peeling and rusted. Despite the efforts of former owner Leon King, Tatassit Beach was auctioned off in June 1995. Robert Saulenas bought it, and he hopes to beautify the area and share it with the public.

TATASSIT LORE ·

It is not widely known, but Tatassit Beach has a most interesting story in its history involving Felix Pollet's nephew, Bob Kane. As a teenager, Kane lived in the Bronx. During the summer, he worked for his uncle at Tatassit Beach. Young Kane loved to draw, so much so that his family was worried that he would waste his life drawing instead of pursuing a career. At Tatassit he spent much of his time drawing pictures of girls at the beach. During a visit to Worcester in 1966, Kane remembered that his Uncle Felix never could figure out how he could afford to go to the movies in Worcester so often, since he came from New York with no money. Later Kane told his uncle that he was taking little "advances" from the concession stand cash register: "Just enough for the bus ride and admission," Kane reminisced.[14]

[14] James A. Gourgouras, "Batman's Creator No Stranger Here," *Worcester Evening Gazette*, March 16, 1966.

An "Airial Chute" was installed at Tatassit Beach. This popular attraction quickly transported swimmers to the water as the T-bar they grasped slid down a cable. (both photos courtesy of Judy Godin)

Locals will be amazed to learn that Bob Kane, the creator of Batman and Robin, once worked for his uncle, Felix Pollet, behind the counter at Tatassit Beach. (illustration courtesy of Judy Godin)

As it turned out, Kane's family should not have worried about his career plans. To this day, the characters he created while he was still a young man have entertained millions of people with their adventures in comic books, on television, and at the movies. Some may be amazed to learn that the creator of Batman and Robin was once behind the counter of the snack bar at Tatassit Beach!

SUNSET BEACH ·

In contrast to the extremely well documented history of Tatassit Beach, very little is known about the story of its "sister," Sunset Beach. Located at the southern end of the lake where Edgemere and the Shrewsbury shore are joined by "Stringer Dam," Sunset Beach has been a popular bathing spot for many, many years. The exact date when it opened as a bathing beach is obscure, but an educated guess might put the date somewhere around 1910, since some of the buildings at the beach have that date written in the cement work. The

beach was first known as "Ecksteadts," named for the family that owned it. It was certainly in operation during the 1920s because a photo in the 1927 Shrewsbury High School yearbook shows a group of students attending a class outing there. In 1928, the founder of Tatassit Beach, Felix Pollet, mentioned that the crowds at Sunset Beach gave him the idea to open his own beach.

The Ecksteadt family sold the beach to Lloyd Anderson in 1943. Anderson's sister, Mrs. Doris Carlson of Storrs, CT, remembers trying to slip unnoticed onto the beach as a child: "We'd sometimes try to swim at Ecksteadt's, but were never allowed to stay, naturally! I guess my brother vowed in those years that he'd buy that beach someday-- and he did!" When Anderson died in 1960, his parents, Olga and Andrew Anderson, acquired the beach. Their daughter and son-in-law, Marilyn (Anderson) Mulcahy and her husband Philip, the current owners, inherited it from them.

Today the beach is much as it was many years ago. Entering the little store at the beach is like stepping back in time fifty years or more. The interior remains virtually the same as it might have looked during World War II, or even earlier. A large stone fireplace is still used, old metal advertising signs line the walls, and Army surplus parachutes are draped from the rafters to form a makeshift ceiling. Patrons can still rent canoes and foot-powered paddle boats; they can picnic, enjoy the swimming areas, and let younger children frolic on a number of playground rides. Even a tall, white diving tower is still used. Mrs. Mulcahy notes that many people who return to the beach as adults always comment that the diving tower looks much higher than it did when they were kids!

All that's missing are the "tubes." These were government surplus thirty-foot rubber boats with the bottoms cut out. Swimmers could dive off, jump on, or bounce into the water from these monsters, which, with a little imagination, resembled great black whales. The only sign of more modern times is a microwave oven used to heat the snacks served to patrons and family alike: the favorite snack

TOBOGGAN
CHUTE
Safety THRILLER
FOR ALL
60 FT. HIGH – 150 FT. LONG
The ONLY ONE *In* MASS.

*The water slide at Tatassit Beach
(both photos courtesy of Judy Godin)*

More than 300 employees of the traffic department of the Worcester office of the New England Telephone & Telegraph Co. (shown sitting on the Toboggan Chute) enjoyed a day of water sports at their annual all-day outing at the Tatassit Canoe Club, Lake Quinsigamond, yesterday. (from the Worcester Daily Telegram, Wednesday, August 28, 1929, reprinted with permission of the Worcester Telegram & Gazette)

Beachgoers at the "kiddie crib" on Tatassit Beach (photo courtesy of Judy Godin) 48

is pizza.

The beach was home to a swimming club for many years, and the numerous awards won by club members are still proudly displayed in the little store. Before Jordan Pond Beach opened, the town's swimming lesson program was conducted at Sunset Beach.

In contrast to the aging relic of Tatassit Beach, Sunset Beach is still well maintained and prosperous. Even today, youth groups from as far away as the Boston area come to the beach to enjoy a day of sun and swimming. Though Sunset Beach didn't have as glamorous a past as Tatassit Beach, it has certainly made up for it in longevity.

The Turner Club, a German social club, is remembered for its tradition of stringing a wire across its landing and hanging three-foot strips of wool soaked in kerosene from it. When the strips were ignited, the wool glowed for long periods during dark summer nights and made a fine display for passing steamboats and canoes. (postcard, author's collection)

~TURNER~CLUB~HOUSE~

-BY-
MN·CONGER.

From the 1870s to the present, social clubs, athletic clubs, and boat clubs have given Lake Quinsigamond a rich social history. Their diversity reflects the various nationalities and economic groups represented in the population of Worcester County.

Starting with the Turn Verein or Turner Club in 1870, these clubs soon began popping up all over the lake area. Many clubs had year-round accommodations in the city. But every May they opened their clubhouses along the shores of the lake, signaling the coming of summer and anticipating a new season of wonderful activities at the lake.

The clubs were either large organizations that stood the test of time or small groups of brief duration. Among the larger clubs were the Turn Verein (or Turner) Club, the Washington Club, Svea Gille, Englebrekt, and the Gesang Verein Frohsinn (or Frohsinn) Club. The smaller clubs included the Frontenac Club, Wapiti (or Elks) Club, English Social Club, Waeuntugs, Rostrevors, Penoke Athletic (or Canoe) Club, Veteran's Fireman Association, Hillside Club, Oghnetas, Octagon Club, Algonquin Canoe Club, Orion Club, and Buzzard's Roost.

For the most part, very little is known about the smaller clubs. The Veteran's Fireman Association and Orion Club occupied King's (sometimes called Sagamore) Point, and the Hillside Club overlooked what was known as Shrewsbury Bay, near 168 South Quinsigamond Avenue. The Penoke Athletic, or Canoe Club, was located just south of the Bigelow estate on South Quinsigamond Avenue. The Waeuntug Club had a three story circular-shaped clubhouse building that stood at Norcross Park, which was located near 115 South Quinsigamond Avenue. With porches circling each story, it looked like a giant wedding cake. The English Social Club, for employees of the Whittall Mills, had its headquarters in south Worcester on Camp Street; however, they did have a clubhouse on the lake in the area of 222 South Quinsigamond Avenue.

The members of the Frontenac and Rostrevor Clubs were, as the names imply, French. Their clubhouses and the Progress Club's clubhouse all stood on Sugarloaf Island at different times. The Wapiti (or Elks) Club on Long Island also had a building on the west shore at Davis Point, or Sandy Bar. In 1900, club members constructed a boardwalk over the docks to reach the clubhouse without getting wet.[1] A small ad informed interested parties that the island was for sale at a club auction in 1905: "This is a rare opportunity to buy the finest island in Lake Quinsigamond for a residence or clubhouse, at your own price."[2]

TURNER CLUB ·

The Turn Verein, or Turner Club, was a German social club whose members were interested in gymnastics. "Turner" in German means a tumbler or gymnast, especially a member of a *turn verein*. The club is remembered for its tradition of stringing a wire across its landing and hanging three-foot strips of wool soaked in kerosene from it. When the strips were ignited, the wool glowed for long periods during dark summer nights and made a fine display for passing steamboats and canoes.[3] The club's quarters were at 206 South Quinsigamond Avenue in Shrewsbury. This building was later home to "Groezinger's," a combination restaurant/ice cream parlor. In the

---

[1] "Mary Ann Tips Over," *Worcester Daily Telegram*, May 1, 1900.

[2] *Worcester Daily Telegram*, April 21, 1905.

[3] Susanna Seymour, "The Lady of the Lake Was a Boat," *Worcester Sunday Telegram*, September 6, 1987.

Washington Club, Lake Quinsigamond. Worcester, Mass.

The Washington Club was formed in Worcester in 1882 by men of Irish descent. It was first called the Washington Square Club or the Irish Catholic Professional Men's Club. (postcard, author's collection)

1940s it became home to the "Lakemen's Lodge," which was used by a group of local residents interested in improving the lake area. The current occupants are the Lithuanian War Veterans, who have made their home there for many years.

WASHINGTON CLUB ·

The Washington Club was formed in Worcester in 1882 by men of Irish descent. It was first called the Washington Square Club or the Irish Catholic Professional Men's Club. Their quarters were at various places in Worcester until a large clubhouse was built in Shrewsbury at 142 South Quinsigamond Avenue in 1887. The new clubhouse was the group's summer quarters.[4] According to club records, the clubhouse was built by Buckley and Elliot and cost $2,785. The club is described in a book published in 1898 by the Worcester Consolidated Street Railway Company:

The Washington Social Club, whose membership consists of young Irish-American citizens, has beautiful grounds and a club house on the Shrewsbury side, and open house is kept throughout the season for its members and lady friends. They also have elegant quarters in the city.[5]

Although reference is made to the club's accessibility to "its members and lady friends," it was many years before women were admitted as members. When families were finally allowed to visit on Sunday afternoons, they could use only certain areas of the club; the members' rooms were strictly off limits. This policy even divided the beach--women and children on one side and men on the other. Only after the club burned down and was rebuilt in the early 1960s were families allowed to use the entire facility.

The fire happened on a night when most of the town's off duty firemen were attending a fireman's ball out of town. By the time the first fire trucks arrived on the scene, the building was engulfed in flames. Private Michael Perna, Sr., now retired, was one of the first firefighters to arrive. Reminiscing today, he describes the fire:

As we were driving to the fire from Shrewsbury center, we could see a glow in the sky. I told my partner, Private Chet Bernard, that we had a good one on our hands. By the time we arrived, the building was already gone. It was so hot that we had to turn our helmets around over our faces to help block the heat. One fire truck that had been located in the club's driveway had to be moved back because of the heat. This was in the fall and it was very dry. The fire started about 6:30 or 7:00 at night. Burning embers flew so far that our neighbor had to wet the roofs of our houses on Oak Street to make sure they didn't catch on fire.

Trees, brush and an adjacent house caught fire. The quick action of Privates Bernard and Perna saved the house. All that remains of the old club is a faded wooden sign on a tree and twin stone pillars flanking the driveway near the entrance on South Quinsigamond Avenue. A low cement block building was erected on the club's site after the fire at a cost of $5,200. Space for tennis, baseball, and hockey, as well as a small golf course, were added to their new quarters; skating and ice fishing also became popular. The club grew so large that its membership was limited to 100.

Mrs. Joanne (Shea) Frew, whose family has belonged to the club for many, many years, remembers growing up at the Washington Club in the 1950s:

---

[4] Frances Green, "Recollections of the Golden Years of the Washington Club," *Worcester Sunday Telegram,* April 23, 1961.

[5] *Picturesque Views on and Adjacent to the Routes of the Worcester Consolidated Street Railway and at Lake Quinsigamond,* Worcester, Mass.: The Worcester Consolidated Street Railway Company, 1898, p. 97.

Men of German descent formed the Gesang Verein Frohsinn, or Frohsinn Club. Their clubhouse was built at 25 North Quinsigamond Avenue in Shrewsbury, where Frohsinn Park once was. (photo reprinted with permission from the Worcester Public Library)

The club was a peaceful place for members and their families to go. We went there almost every day during the summer. There never was, and still isn't, a telephone, so you couldn't be reached there. There was never any open drinking of liquor. The members didn't want any drunkenness or yelling, although once in a while someone might get a little carried away at playing cards. We never thought much about the strict rules, it was just the way it was. A certain decorum was expected.

Everyone knew everyone else and watched out for them. There were no lifeguards to watch the children, but all the adults kept a close eye on them. There have never been any hot water showers at the club. Some of the men would get out of work, come to the club and lather up in the lake. It was quite a sight. Then they would take a swim, finishing up with a cold water shower.

Some athletes among the members were well known: E. J. Kerns was a pioneer in the sport of crew racing on the lake and coached the first local crew of national rowing champions; J. Fred Powers was an all-American decathlon champion; John Reid and Dr. John J. Kelly were well known runners; and Major Frank Kavanaugh was the "Iron Major" of football coaching fame.[6]

Two popular social events were the annual Washington Ball – first held at Mechanics Hall or Horticultural Hall and later at the Bancroft Hotel – and an annual Field Day with races and ball games, tugs of war, a shore dinner, and Irish songs and dances. Playing cards was a favorite activity. In a 1961 interview, one of the older club members recalled, "the widowers and bachelors sometimes played cards until almost morning. Then they'd walk back to the

city, going to church on the way, and get home just in time for breakfast."[7]

The club's membership had dwindled to roughly forty members and their families before the property was sold to a private party in October 1996.

FROHSINN CLUB AND THE BUZZARD'S ROOST · · · · · · · ·

Descendants of German immigrants formed the Gesang Verein Frohsinn, or Frohsinn Club. Their clubhouse was built at 25 North Quinsigamond Avenue in Shrewsbury, where Frohsinn Park once was. The original building was destroyed by a fire in March 1936, but the group rebuilt at the same location by July of the same year. The Frohsinn Club is still very active and their quarters are available for all types of functions.

The Buzzard's Roost was, along with the Frohsinn Club, one of the few clubs on the northern part of the lake. Their building, a cottage, was located off Fifth Avenue, which runs off North Quinsigamond Avenue. Though a small group, they were apparently very active. A 1925 newspaper article describes their preparations for the upcoming Fourth of July holiday:

Members of the Buzzard's Roost, the most active club at the northern end of the lake and leaders in the annual night before celebration in the vicinity of Lincoln Park and the White City, will continue the yearly custom with an elaborate plan of entertainment this season. In addition to conducting its annual night before party and dance, it is planned to conduct a horribles parade at the lake providing a suitable number of clubs will collaborate. On the holi-

---

[6] Frances Green, "Recollections of the Golden Years of the Washington Club," *Worcester Sunday Telegram,* April 23, 1961.

[7] Ibid.

Svea Gille Club, Lake
Quinsigamond.
WORCESTER, Mass.

Residents of Swedish heritage founded the Svea Gille Club in 1888. Their clubhouse was a huge, imposing structure located on South Quinsigamond Avenue at the intersection of Oak Street. The building was three stories high with turrets reaching up even higher. (postcard, author's collection)

day the members will have a series of water events with many of the Boys' Club male and female swimming stars as contestants.[8]

SVEA GILLE ·

The Svea Gille was formed in 1888 by local residents of Swedish heritage. Its clubhouse was a huge, imposing structure located on South Quinsigamond Avenue at the intersection of Oak Street. The building was three stories high with tall turrets reaching up even higher. A wide stairway led down to a boat landing at the water's edge. The lakeside clubhouse was described in a 1919 Worcester history:

The club house of the society is located at the southeast end of Lake Quinsigamond. The foundations were laid with much ceremony May 30, 1894, and the house completed that year at a cost of $8,000. The society has 15 acres of land. The house is one of the largest and best equipped at the lake.[9]

Svea Gille was sold in the 1960s and became the home of the Ancient Order of Hibernians. In 1979, as the Quinsigamond Athletic Club, it had a small pub which served food and drinks; the rest of the building was used as a function facility. It was sold to developers and demolished in 1987. The Lake View Condominiums now stand on the site. The two huge fieldstone pillars that stood facing the street denoting the name Svea Gille, one with an "S" and the other with a "G," were still in place up to the time the building was razed. One of them now stands on privately-owned Blake Island as a monument to lake days gone by.

ENGLEBREKT CLUB ·

The Englebrekt Club, another Swedish organization, was one of the longest lasting clubs at the lake. Their lake quarters were in the

building that still stands at 181 Lake Avenue in Worcester. A column in the *Worcester Telegram* on July 1, 1925 entitled "At the Lake" describes the club:

The Englebrekt club, Lake Avenue, is one of the numerous large Swedish clubs at the lake. It is three and a half stories high. It is open each day in the year for members and guests with an experienced chef in attendance at all times. In addition to its home-like atmosphere the club furnishes an ideal place for swimming as there is a large wharf bordering on the lake front.

The July 4th program includes plans to cover every minute from the night before celebration until midnight of the holiday. Open house will be in order and following a midnight supper on the Third the members will dance until daylight, with a special orchestra furnishing music.

The club was organized about 35 years ago and the clubhouse was built three or four years later. David Hulmquist is president and he will take charge of the holiday celebrations.

The club existed until 1976, operating as a restaurant and function facility. Then the building was taken over by its current owner, the Marine Corps League.

LATER CLUBS ·

Years later, other clubs appeared on the scene. These included the Lakemen's Lodge, Three Acres Park, Olympia Park, and Maironis Park.

The Lakemen's Lodge was organized in 1937 by a group of Shrewsbury's lake area residents, many of Italian descent, who felt put

---

8 "Buzzard's Roost Will Celebrate," *Worcester Daily Telegram*, July 1, 1925.

9 Charles Nutt, A. B., *History of Worcester and Its People*, New York: Lewis Historical Publishing Company, 1919, p. 363.

The Frontenac Club, circa 1898 (photo reprinted with permission from the Worcester Public Library)

upon by the town government and the people at the "Center." Their first meeting was called to order by none other than Anthony "Spag" Borgatti, who gave a short talk outlining the goals of group. Members pursued political offices and helped to better the lake area. Within a few years their numbers and political clout had grown considerably, making the group a force to be reckoned with in town affairs.

Their first meetings were held in the basement of St. Anne's Church, then in a small building on the turnpike. Later they were held in a portable schoolhouse building at what is now a residence at 3 Lakewood Drive on Jordan Pond. In 1946, they acquired the Turner Club's clubhouse on the lake. Seven years later, when some members were recalled to the armed forces during the Korean War, they sold the clubhouse to the Lithuanian War Veterans. For a short time in 1952, the club was known as the "Club Ship Ahoy."[10]

In addition to its political activities, the group was well known for its dances, minstrel shows, and other social affairs. After many years the group became largely inactive, having achieved their original goals. They sponsored a scholarship for high school students each year until 1984. The group members, now mostly in their seventies and eighties, had one last big bash in September 1996 to officially close the club.

The Three Acres Park, Lithuanian Naturalization and Social Club, Olympia Park and Maironis Park were all groups for people of Lithuanian descent. For a number of years, Olympia Park and Three Acres Park were rumored to have "Communists" as members; the Three Acres Park in particular was known in local circles as the "Commie Club." During World War II, some Shrewsbury town employees were asked to keep an eye on the club for any "suspicious activities." As far as anyone knows, no "suspicious activities" have occurred at either location, before or since. The Three Acres Park is still located at 67 North Quinsigamond Avenue and has a small membership.

Olympia Park was on the site of the Eyrie Hotel before burning in the mid-1970s. It was well known for ballroom dancing through the 1930s and '40s, and also had an open-air dance pavilion. During the 1930s, the club was restricted to members only. This did not prevent young Lithuanian girls from giving young non-Lithuanian boys the secret Lithuanian password that would allow them to get past the guard at the door, however.

Maironis Park is located at 52 South Quinsigamond Avenue in Shrewsbury, on a section of the Bigelows' vast property. This land was purchased by a group of shareholders in 1923 and the grand opening of the park was May 30, 1924. The park was named for the great Lithuanian poet and patriot, J. Maironis, and provided a place for local Lithuanian groups to have picnics and family outings. By 1925 the park was losing money and many of the original shareholders withdrew. By 1929 the park was sold to another group, the Lithuanian Charitable Society. This group hoped to build a home for the elderly on the site, but they were unable to get the necessary permits. The existing building, which had been the Bigelows' barn, was then renovated as a clubhouse and picnics and outings once again became popular. Following World War II a new wave of Lithuanian immigrants increased the organization's membership.[11]

The clubhouse underwent a major expansion in 1968, when another hall was added, along with a member's room, a new kitchen, and a renovated lounge. Due to increasing membership, another addition was begun in 1973. However, on Christmas Eve of that year a disastrous fire leveled the club and the nearly completed addition.[12] The fire, although destructive, almost ended in a greater tragedy. When it was almost completely out, two firemen were wetting down

---

[10] "Lithuanian Vets Purchase Lakemen's Lodge," *Worcester Evening Gazette*, August 25, 1953.

[11] Jack Tubert, "90 Year Old Recalls Maironis Park of Old," *Worcester Telegram and Gazette*, December 9, 1974. Also see dedication pamphlet for the new Maironis Park building, April 1975.

[12] Ibid.

On Lake Quinsigamond, Worcester, Mass.

The Rostrevor Club (postcard, author's collection)

the ruins from an aerial ladder. A mechanical failure tipped the ladder truck, dropping the extended ladder just feet above the smoldering ruins. Luckily the flames had died down, otherwise the two firemen would have met with an untimely end. They were able to make their way back down the ladder to safety, with no major injuries. Club members were determined to rebuild, however, and by December 1974 they were proud to celebrate the grand opening of a new clubhouse that is still in operation today.

The Lithuanian Naturalization and Social Club was located on Davis Way, off of Lake Avenue. This peninsula, which was once the shore-side location of the Wapiti Club and later the Algonquin Canoe Club, is really a part of Shrewsbury. The original building, known as the Bungalow, was purchased in 1913 as the club's summer quarters, although the downtown quarters were also open year-round. The original building was replaced by a larger one in 1922. This building burned down in 1930 and was rebuilt. Popular activities included fishing and dancing. However, in its last years the clubhouse was not a profitable venture. It burned again in 1972, and the site is now a private residence.[13]

The Wapiti Club
(reprinted with permission from the Worcester Public Library)

13 "Lithuanian Club Sets Anniversary Banquet," *Worcester Telegram and Gazette*, December 1, 1973.

Jesse Johnson Coburn opened Lincoln Park as the first recreation complex at the lake. It became a place where people could picnic, take a steamboat ride from the nearby landing, rent a boat or canoe, and enjoy a variety of rides and games. It was immensely popular, and as the years passed, a large theatre (background), a dance hall, and a carousel were added to the park. (photo courtesy of Michael Paika)

EARLY DAYS OF LEISURE AT LINCOLN PARK

The first great step in the creation of what would become the huge recreation complex at Lake Quinsigamond was the brainchild of Jesse Johnson Coburn. Born in Northfield, Vermont in 1832, Coburn went to California at age eighteen as one of the forty-niners in the gold rush. He returned a few years later after many exciting adventures in the mining towns and worked in the scrap metal business in Worcester.[1]

J. J. Coburn was one of the first people to consider the possibilities of developing the lake into a recreation spot. He bought Ramshorn Island, just off the causeway, and built the Quinsigamond House Hotel there in 1867. At about the same time, he started running steamboats up and down the lake.

He also bought the land at the southwest corner of the causeway and developed it gradually over the next several years. At various times it was known as Quinsigamond Grove, Coburn's Grove and finally Lincoln Park. Coburn made this spot the first amusement park area at the lake. Described in a brochure a few years later, Coburn cleared away the underbrush and installed "seats, swings, flying horses, refreshment booths and dance pavilions." He later built a "refreshment saloon" and bowling alley.[2]

The "Dummy" railroad had its terminus at the entrance to the park and provided quick, cheap transportation to and from Lincoln Park. An "omnibus" also transported people to the park in the early days. One of the first attractions at the park was Thomas Edison's

"more or less recently perfected phonograph, [which] did its cylindrical whirl of song or recitation at five cents per, through a stethoscope-like apparatus."[3]

Lincoln Park had become a place where people could picnic, take a steamboat ride from the nearby landing, rent a boat or canoe, and enjoy a variety of rides and games. It was immensely popular with the people of Worcester and vicinity. As the years passed, a large theatre, a dance hall, and a carousel were added to the park.

At the "Casino" one could purchase a variety of refreshments. In the mid-1920s, "old timers" remembered some of the treats:

> *Gosh wasn't that swell vanilla ice cream they had? And what sandwiches! Who said boiled live lobster? What ho, ice cold tonic at five cents a man-sized glass! It doesn't seem possible; but there it was, anything your heart desired from "little daisy" to sarsaparilla.*[4]

A "prominent attraction" for lake visitors was surely a novelty to young and old alike--a live alligator. "Mr. Coburn's alligator," as it was known, had "just arrived from the Everglades." The monster was ten feet long and described in the *Worcester Evening Gazette:*

> *[Mr. Coburn's alligator is] by far the best specimen of his tribe ever seen in this vicinity....He is confined on the shore of the Lake, with access to the water, and is a genuine curiosity. Visitors should remember, however, that the creature is none the better for being punched*

---

[1] Charles Nutt, A. B., *History of Worcester and Its People,* New York: Lewis Historical Publishing Co., 1919, pp. 750-51.

[2] Edward R. Fiske, *Pleasure Resorts in Worcester County,* Worcester, MA, 1877, pp. 13-15.

[3] James H. Powers, "Many Changes at the Lake in the Last Thirty Years," *Worcester Evening Post,* July 10, 1926.

[4] Ibid.

Skating Rink and Hall, Lincoln Park, Worcester, Mass.

In 1905 Lincoln Park added a roller skating rink to update the park and to compete with the newly opened White City amusement park. (postcard, author's collection)

with rails, and can be seen to better advantage if left to himself.... All who take the trip to the lake this summer will want to see this amphibious monster. [5]

Over the years, many traveling vaudeville shows performed at the theatre. In August 1907, J. W. Gorman's "Alabama Troubadours" appeared in what had become an annual event. The *Worcester Evening Post* announced one program: "A carnival of Darktown Jollity, A Brilliant Medly *[sic]* of Plantation Pastimes [featuring] Chocolate Belles, Jubilee Singers, Coon Town Songs, A Galaxy of Colored Stars, Buck and Wing Dancers [and] familiar plantation melodies, that none but the southern darkies know how to sing." Appearing at the same time, on a fifty-foot stage constructed especially for the show, were "Vallecita's Leopards," which featured five leopards in an "immense cage." This part of the show was free to the public.[6] Other examples of the wide variety of acts that appeared at the park include "The Miltons--Sensational Upside Down Equilibrists," "Reed's Acrobatic Bull Terriers, Featuring the Wonderful English Whippet Somersault Dog 'Dixie,'" and "Faust and Faust, Panomimic Comedians."[7]

The dance hall near "Harry Cocaine's hot dog stand" on the Belmont Street side of the park featured big name bands during this era. As its management changed, its name changed, but it was probably best known as the "Coconut Grove." In 1905, the bowling alley was superseded by a roller skating rink in an effort to update the park due to the opening of the White City amusement park.[8] Various advertisements promoted the new roller skating rink: "Do you Skate?" "Visit the Lincoln Park Skating Rink," "Three Sessions Daily, Sunday Excepted," "Good Skates," "Excellent Floor," "Free Instructions to Beginners."

Like its "sister" park, White City, Lincoln Park also had special attractions. These included high divers, acrobats, sword swallowers, wild west shows, and, of course, wild animals. Elephants visited the park at least once: photos show a number of pachyderms enjoying a swim in the lake and emerging from the water with throngs of spectators standing nearby.

A good description of one of the popular high diving acts appeared in the *Worcester Daily Telegram* on June 18, 1905. This particular act was chosen to attract patrons drawn to the newly opened White City, and was offered free of charge.

The Norins, Oscar and Siri, will give high diving stunts at the park every afternoon at 2:30 o'clock and every night at 9:30 o'clock. The Norins are famous high divers. They showed at the New England fair two years ago. In 1894 three brothers did the diving. Oscar, the eldest, was the highest diver, going down at Lakewood park from a height of 90 feet. Two of the brothers were killed, and since then the diving is done by the man and woman.

Oscar makes a fire dive in which he wears a suit of paper saturated with gasoline to which a torch is applied before he leaves the platform. He wears an asbestos suit under his diving suit.

In an extremely detailed account which follows, John Cumming, who grew up near the lake, provides a "snapshot" of Lincoln Park and its attractions during the 1920s and later. We are indebted to him for sharing his memories with us.

Cumming vividly remembers a number of concession stands offering games of chance or skill. These included various types of ball

5 "At the Lake," *Worcester Evening Gazette*, July 6, 1880.

6 "Lincoln Park," *Worcester Evening Post*, August 3, 1907.

7 Undated program, author's collection.

8 "Ten Alleys at the Lake," *Worcester Evening Gazette*, April 25, 1905.

Elephants visited Lincoln Park at least once. This photo shows a group of pachyderms emerging from the lake after a swim and delighting many spectators. (photo courtesy of J. Ronald Bigelow)

throwing, balloon-popping and ring-tossing games. One, called the Chinese rolling ball, was operated by a person he describes as "Taki Kamur, an excitable Japanese" (a 1921 newspaper ad spells his name Take Kimura). Cumming explains the game itself: "Large ornate displays of fancy dishes from China and Japan enticed participants to roll rubber balls along a miniature bowling alley in hopes of winning a dish or two. Some came back regularly in an effort to fill out a whole set of dishes."

This particular stand was divided into two parts. The other part was a shooting gallery where players shot cork-firing air rifles at pyramids of cigarette packages, including Lucky Strikes, Camels, Sweet Caporals, and exotic Turkish brands, which were also the prizes, according to Cumming. In an amusing sidelight to this story, Cumming describes how what he calls "park urchins" would sometimes draw the game operator's ire:

They would crouch down below the counter, quickly seize an air rifle, pop the cork and run. In an instant Taki Kamur would vault the counter in hot pursuit, shouting unintelligible epithets at the scoundrels. Before he had run very far, he would pull up suddenly and return to his unattended stand.

Cumming recalls another booth which featured a real shooting gallery with .22 caliber rifles: "A row of tiny white ducks would move across the rear of the gallery, falling over as they were hit. No prizes were offered here; it was truly a game of skill. An exceptional marksman attracted a large group of admiring spectators."

A penny arcade contained a number of machines, including some that created early motion pictures when the operator turned a crank that flipped photos in rapid succession, much as a child might do with a series of stick figures drawn on bits of paper to create a primitive cartoon. Cumming tells of another attraction that was a bit more shocking:

...the brave could test their manhood by grasping two electrically charged posts which, when moved apart, increased the current. A colorful chart indicated the degree of manhood represented by the various positions of the posts. The youngsters soon discovered that by joining hands several could share the benefits of a single penny.

Of course, some performers used the allure of magic and mystery to entertain. Cumming remembers one of these in particular:

Along the midway there were often itinerants who came for a few weeks or a season to guess weights or tell fortunes. One of the latter functions was performed by a dusky, turbaned Hindu, who inserted a blank sheet of paper into a glass tube and held it up before him as he shouted mysterious incantations in a strange language. Occasionally he passed the glass tube over a flame. Finally he would remove the sheet of paper from the tube and proudly display it to the crowd, pointing to the writing which had appeared on what had been a blank sheet of paper. The park urchins listened to the incantations so often that they succeeded in memorizing the ritual. Much to the Hindu's irritation, they would recite the incantations in chorus with him. He always conveyed the impression that he could speak no English, but one of the little eavesdroppers heard him talking in perfect English with one of the park proprietors.

The many hot dog concessions on the western side of Lake Avenue also remain stamped on Cumming's memory: "They were usually besieged with crowds of hungry customers. Mountains of hot dogs were consumed at five cents each." Of these stands, one called "Corey's" existed well into recent times. Anyone who ever had one of their delicious hot dogs served in a steamed roll will understand why John Cumming finds it so easy to remember these "dogs"!

The biggest day of the year at Lincoln Park was the Fourth of July. Once again, Cumming provides a vivid "start to finish" account

OPEN AIR THEATRE, LAKE QUINSIGAMOND, WORCESTER, MASS.

The Open Air Theatre at Lincoln Park (postcard, author's collection)

of the activities at the park, making the firecrackers almost audible and the brilliant fireworks almost visible:

> *Fourth of July was the night of all nights at Lincoln Park. The crowded street cars began to arrive early on the evening of the third. The youngsters in the neighborhoods around the park were given complete freedom that night; at least the boys were. The young boys, many in the twelve-year-old or younger range, would approach the park singing in somewhat discordant chorus, "We won't be home until morning. We won't be home until morning. It's the night before the fourth." Even after the night's activities were over, the youngsters would linger on, refusing to go home until daylight.*

> *The revellers made lots of noise on the night before the Fourth. Horns, bells, firecrackers, cap pistols, and every conceivable noise maker was used. Firecrackers were tossed helter-skelter about, often at a person's feet. Some carried canes which had a cap detonating device at the bottom. Each time it was struck against the ground it emitted a pistol-like noise. Firecrackers came in a variety of sizes from the tiny "baby-fingers," which were ignited in strips, to the cannon crackers or "four-inchers." The latter were considered dangerous and were illegal. From time to time, however, one heard one of these law-breakers exploding, louder than all the others. The urchins kept a sharp eye open for the firecracker that proved to be a dud. They picked them up and broke them open to ignite the gun powder. In spite of such reckless use of fireworks, few injuries resulted.*

> *The evening reached its climax at midnight. At that time everyone gathered at the waterfront to watch the brilliant display of fireworks on Thule Island. There were pinwheels, waterfalls, and many other clever arrangements, interspersed with volleys of rockets which, when bursting in the air far above the water, lighted up the whole area. At such times one could see a mass of canoes and boats gunwale to gunwale. Every inch of ground at the park waterfront was occupied; and no open space on the lake in that area remained.*

During the 1930s Lincoln Park began to wither away. Even though the dance hall remained popular, one by one the rides and other attractions were closed, until all that remained were the skating rink, the hotel and the dance hall. Eventually even these remnants disappeared. In 1961, the dance hall, which had been so popular during the "glory days" of the park and had recently hosted "[record hops] which were held in an effort to attract business," burned almost to the ground.[9] A few years later the Lincoln Park Hotel, which had wasted away to a neighborhood tavern and boarding house, was also damaged by fire and subsequently torn down.

The once great amusement complex at Lincoln Park is no more. Gone are the steamboat docks, the boat houses, the rides, amusements and refreshment stands. Today the high rise elderly apartment complex that occupies most of this site gives no hint of the crowds of fun-seekers that thronged to the amusement park many years ago.

---

9 "Flames Dance Lakeside Finale," *Worcester Evening Gazette,* April 29, 1961.

The Worcester and Shrewsbury Railroad was more popularly known as the "Dummy" railroad because the locomotives were disguised to look like horsecars so they wouldn't frighten any horses that might see them. (photo from the collections of the Worcester Historical Museum, circa 1880)

A Ride on the "Dummy": The Worcester and Shrewsbury Railroad

By January 1873, a group headed by J. J. Coburn responded to the need for a quick and inexpensive way to transport people from the city to the growing resort area at Lake Quinsigamond. They began investigating the possibility of constructing a railroad from the city to the lake. The result was a somewhat miniature, narrow-gauge railroad with only three feet between the rails. Named the Worcester and Shrewsbury Railroad, (W&SRR) it was more popularly known as the "Dummy" railroad.[1] The unusual name "Dummy" was coined because the locomotives were disguised to look like horsecars so they wouldn't frighten any horses that might see them. This was only partially successful--on at least one occasion, a horse was frightened, ran into another team of horses, and the rider was thrown "violently to the ground."[2]

Construction began in May 1873 and the little train made its first trip to the lake on July 31 of that year. The Dummy was one of the first narrow-gauge roads in the eastern part of the United States and was so successful that it became the model for a number of others.[3] An ad published shortly after the line was completed announced the train's schedule: "From April to November, every Hour from 6:30 A.M. to 9:30 P.M. Every other hour during the Winter Months. FARE, - - TEN CENTS."[4]

The entire length of the railroad was only 2.7 miles, although extending the line into Shrewsbury as far as the center of town was considered as early as 1875. The *Shrewsbury News* reported on a meeting that took place on February 24, where James Draper, treasurer of the railroad, discussed the expansion plans. The vote was forty-two in favor, two opposed. A survey was completed regarding the proposal to extend the line through Northborough as far as Marlborough.[5] The merits of these extensions were debated on a number of occasions over the years.

In his diary, Josiah Stone, a long-time Shrewsbury resident, mentions the discussions relating to extending the line into Shrewsbury in a number of entries. Stone's diary entry for March 29, 1882 states that a vote was taken at the Town Meeting to see if the town should take stock in the amount of $15,000 to support the extension of the Dummy with the following results: "The vote on this question as declared by the Moderator this day 112 yes 95 no. not a two thirds vote as required [sic]."[6]

The subject arose again three years later. Mr. Stone's diary entry, dated March 2, 1885, mentions the Town Meeting vote on "the question of having the Town aid to the extent of fifteen thousand dollars to extend the Worcester and Shrewsbury Dummy R. Road to Shrewsbury. 114 yea 109 nay." Again, no two thirds majority, therefore no Dummy to Shrewsbury. Mr. Stone attends Town Meeting on September 21 of the same year and reports, "a full meeting, much enthusiasm for a narrow gauge R. Road from the Lake to Main Street."[7]

---

[1] Edward R. Fiske, *Pleasure Resorts in Worcester County*, Worcester, MA, 1877, pp. 29-33.

[2] *Shrewsbury News*, September 28, 1877.

[3] Fiske, pp. 29-33.

[4] Worcester City Directory, 1873.

[5] *Shrewsbury News*, March 5, 1875.

[6] *Josiah Goddard Stone Diary*, from the Collection of the Old Sturbridge Village Research Library.

[7] Ibid.

The railroad company itself showed continued interest in proceeding with the extension, according to Mr. Stone's diary entry on October 22, 1885: "The rout for the long talk'd of Dummy Railroad is being surveyed over my farm to day--this is the 4th or 5th time the way has been surveyed since the road from Worcester to the Lake [was built] *[sic]*." Despite much enthusiasm, the town of Shrewsbury never approved the expenditure for the railroad extension.[8]

The Dummy line began in Worcester, where a little depot stood near Union Station. It then proceeded roughly a half mile to Draper's Station, which was the first stop for outbound trains. The halfway point of the line was Bloomingdale Station on Plantation Street. The Dummy track in this area overlooked the Boston and Albany tracks which ran through the "Deep Cut": "this great thoroughfare of the iron horse as they thunder through deep cut passageways, walled in on either side by the abrupt faces of the natural ledge, down which little streams trickle, and in the crevices of which dwarf vegetation has found a footing."[9]

The Deep Cut is still in use today. From the Plantation Street bridge which crosses it, it becomes readily apparent why the Dummy line was routed around it: there simply was not enough room for the little train or its tracks to fit through this narrow passage. In 1937 at age 85, Edgar Goodwill, an engineer on the Dummy, recalled the Blizzard of 1888. He was aboard the Dummy with seven passengers and the snow came down so hard, "you had to cut it to get ahead." When they reached the Deep Cut, there were fifteen-foot drifts and six regular trains stuck there. After the cars were disconnected from the little engine, Goodwill and his passengers proceeded as best they could until the Dummy engine left the tracks near Putnam Lane and hit a fence. They all made it home despite the snow and the crash, but Goodwill had strained himself trying to keep the line open through the drifts and left his job with the Dummy.[10]

From the Deep Cut, the Dummy's tracks wound down the hill towards the lake, running through the then-new neighborhood called Lake View, until reaching the end of the line. It was here, near the entrance to Lincoln Park on what is now Lake Avenue, that another station stood, along with a small maintenance building and a turntable used to turn the engines around for their trip back to the city.[11]

The W&SRR started off with three engines, two Dummy engine cars and a more conventional-looking locomotive named the "E. B. Stoddard" after the President of the line.[12] The growing popularity of the resort areas at the lake soon necessitated adding more cars, however. By 1878, a long covered car and three open cars were added to the line; the latter were particularly popular during warmer weather.[13] Dummy engine #1 and its open trailer car were called the "Quinsigamond Lake."

The W&SRR proved to be a great improvement over previous means of reaching the lake from the city by 1877: "it had in great part supplanted all other means of conveyance to and from the lake, and its liberal patronage is attested by the statistics of the road which show that annually since its opening, from 110,000 to 150,000 passengers have been carried over the route." This same source notes that on July 4, 1877 the train carried no less than 5,690 passengers.[14]

After ten years of operation, Horace H. Bigelow bought the rail-

---

[8] Ibid.

[9] Fiske, pp. 29-33.

[10] "Lake Quinsigamond Has Gone 'Sissy' Says Steamboater of Fifty Years Ago," *Sunday Telegram*, January 10, 1937.

[11] Fiske, pp. 29-33.

[12] Ibid.

[13] Ibid. Also see the *Shrewsbury News*, May 10 and May 17, 1878.

[14] Fiske, pp. 29-33.

road as part of his plan to expand the lake area. By 1890, business had grown so much that the railroad was running eighteen round trips daily in the winter and twenty-two in the summer, with four to six extra trips almost daily. The capacity of the line at this point was roughly two thousand people per hour. In 1890 the railroad had twelve pieces of equipment: four locomotives, two each of fifteen and thirty tons, and eight cars.

A ride on the Dummy left a great impression on its passengers. One Worcester resident, Mrs. Dorothy L. Salter, remembered riding the Dummy in an interview with the *Worcester Sunday Telegram* in 1968: "I remember, it was narrow gauge, with a little locomotive. The little cars were red. I suppose it must have been smoky--but you didn't notice that when you were little."[15] Perhaps the best description of the excitement can be found in an article entitled "Many Changes at Lake in the Last Thirty Years," which appeared in the *Worcester Evening Post* on July 10, l926: "Will you ever forget the 'kick' you got out of your Sunday afternoon ride down to the Lake on the 'Dummy' train and the way your heart thumped as your youthful eye caught the white canvas sails of the skiffs as they danced on the billows?...Recall that you could hardly wait for the train to chatter to a stop that you might rush pell mell down to the hobby horses for a mechanical canter?"

After the Dummy was modernized to standard gauge and electrified in 1893, the trolleys served the same purpose as the Dummy for many years. Somehow though, it must have been different. In 1896, the Dummy was leased to the Worcester Consolidated Street Railway. The Dummy was then replaced by trolleys and its station became the Lincoln Park Hotel. John Cumming, a Shrewsbury native, remembers the trolleys at Lincoln Park:

> [They] disgorged passengers by the scores throughout the summer. On a busy weekend evening a double line of open summer trolley cars a quarter of a mile in length would extend from the end of the tracks to the car barn awaiting the mass exodus which would take place around midnight. The revellers came from all over Worcester and on weekends from as far off as Boston.

Finally replaced by busses in the late 1920s, the Dummy line ceased operations along with most of Worcester's trolley services.[16]

Above: Tickets for one passage to or from Lake Quinsigamond on the Worcester and Shrewsbury Railroad (author's collection)

---

[15] Polly Lindi, "When Venus Was Queen of the Lake," *Sunday Telegram*, August 25, 1968.

[16] Stephen P. Carlson and Thomas W. Harding, *Worcester Trolleys Remembered*, Worcester Regional Transit Authority, 1985, p. 8.

An artist's depiction of the White City amusement park: notice the "Shoot-the-Chutes" ride, the scenic railway, and the "Flying Airships." (White City pamphlet, circa 1907, author's collection)

THE WHITE CITY AMUSEMENT PARK: "FIFTY THOUSAND ELECTRIC LIGHTS"

In the early part of the twentieth century, the great businessman and Lake Quinsigamond developer, Horace H. Bigelow, had a dream to construct a giant amusement park on the shores of the lake that would be the most modern and exciting anywhere. H. H. Bigelow was the one for this job. Throughout his life he had achieved one success after another in the business world. Primarily involved in the shoemaking business and other types of manufacturing, Bigelow also invented and built machines that were used in many factories at the turn of the century.[1]

With his fortune made, Bigelow turned to real estate development as his next venture. Eventually he became one of the best known men in the city of Worcester and one of its largest real estate owners. Bigelow was also a civic-minded individual who was quick to support causes that would result in "the betterment of social conditions and the beautifying of the city."[2] He was not easily swayed from his course, and at times "knocked heads" with those who did not share his views.

His stubbornness sometimes led to disputes with the city leaders. One of the most well known episodes involved Bigelow's Rink, a huge building used for roller skating and exhibitions, which he bought in 1881 from financially troubled owners who had hosted roller skating tailored to the privileged upper classes there. Bigelow added scenic gardens and fountains after buying the property.[3] Worcester's Centrum Centre stands on the site of this building, in the area of Mechanic and Foster streets, and serves a similar purpose to its predecessor.

In his efforts to provide entertainment for the common man, Bigelow lowered prices at the roller skating emporium, which by all accounts was greatly successful. All of a sudden, people who had never roller skated were flying around the rink with varying degrees of success. On one particular Saturday night, 700 people visited the rink. Towards the end of the evening the skaters became more reckless, which "induced a repeated number of falls and pick ups, and afforded happy opportunities for an exhibition of sportive gallantry toward the fair ones on the part of the experienced skaters." Bigelow eventually operated five roller skating rinks throughout New England.[4]

When he opened his first rink, the Sunday "blue laws" were much stricter than they are today. Bigelow wanted the average family to enjoy their day off, so he decided to hold a series of Sunday concerts starting in July 1882. Many people were appalled: one of the city's churches complained to city hall, and the second Sunday concert was shut down shortly after it began.[5]

As a result, Bigelow was hauled into court, lost the case and fined twenty dollars. He appealed the decision and used the trial to draw attention to his cause. By the time the trial reached the Supreme Judicial Court in 1884, the city dropped the case because Sunday had become a popular day of recreation.

---

[1] Charles Nutt, A. B., *History of Worcester and Its People*, New York: Lewis Historical Publishing Co., 1919, pp. 769-71.

[2] Ibid.

[3] "Bigelow's Garden," *Worcester Evening Gazette*, July 28, 1882 and "Sunday Concerts," *Worcester Evening Gazette*, July 31, 1882.

[4] "Saturday Night at the Rink," *Worcester Evening Gazette*, April 11, 1882.

[5] *Worcester Evening Gazette*, July 31, 1882.

Worcester, Mass.
Lake Quinsigamond.
The White City.
Main Entrance.

The gates at the White City amusement park officially opened to their first crowd of pleasure seekers on June 18, 1905, a sweltering summer Sunday. (postcard, author's collection)

A crowd of merry makers at White City amusement park, which opened in 1905 and closed forever fifty-five years later on Labor Day 1960. (White City pamphlet, circa 1907, author's collection)

THE BAY STATE "LIMITED" AT WHITE CITY, WORCESTER, MASS.

The "Miniature Railway" was exactly what it claimed to be: the locomotive was only five feet long and twenty-eight inches high. The engine used miniature pieces of coal and the owners hired midgets as the conductor and engineer. (postcard, author's collection)

Bigelow's other interest at the time was electricity. He saw to it that his roller skating rink was lit with arc lights powered by an on site generating station. He promoted electricity to the public and later hosted exhibitions featuring electrically powered machines, including an "electric car," which would soon become a common sight as trolleys replaced horses as a means of transportation.[6] Bigelow's fascination with electricity would play a part in his opening the White City amusement park a few years later: one of his advertising slogans for the event touted, "Fifty Thousand Electric Lights!"[7]

By 1904, Bigelow was ready to make his dream happen. He had plans designed for the White City amusement park, which would occupy the site of his "Quinsigamond Forest" just east of the causeway. In the spring of 1905 his project was gaining momentum: in March, representatives from the Dreamland Company arrived from New York to help design the park. Their company helped design the well-known Dreamland at Coney Island as well as White City amusement parks all over the country.[8] Eventually more than forty parks would take the name White City, which originated from a popular attraction at the 1893 Chicago World's Fair (not from the white-painted buildings).[9]

An ambitious schedule was set for the park's completion. The builders anticipated that an extensive network of boardwalks would be completed within one week. After setting an opening date of May 27, 1905, they decided that the park could open even earlier, on May 20.[10] Accordingly, advertising cards were printed showing an artist's exaggerated conception of the finished park on one side, with too many rides and buildings, and listing brief descriptions of many of the attractions on the reverse.[11]

As the date drew closer, opening day was extended to May 27. Construction moved along quickly until May 2. On this particular day, the business agent for the local carpenter's union called on the roughly 120 carpenters employed on the project to go on strike. In their haste to meet the opening day deadline, the management hired some non-union carpenters to help out, thereby incurring the union's wrath.[12]

The business agent had been "pestering" the carpenters to strike and trying to speak with the superintendent of the job, who had avoided him so far. That morning he finally resorted to threatening his own union members with fifty-dollar fines if they returned to work. About half heeded his warning and went on strike. The agent attempted to convince the rest of the laborers to join the striking carpenters, but they kept on working.[13]

By one o'clock the same day, some of the striking carpenters had returned to work. They may have been swayed by the superintendent's reasoning that he would be happy to hire union carpenters exclusively, but only if he could find enough to allow him to open the park on time. If not, he would seek out whoever could fill the demand. Further, he said that he was perfectly willing to talk to any union official, "provided the man knows what he is talking about and can walk straight about the park."[14] (It was rumored that the business agent spent a good deal of time in a tipsy state.)

---

[6] Nutt, pp. 769-71.

[7] "The White City, Lake Quinsigamond, Worcester, Massachusetts," 1907, courtesy of Michael Paika.

[8] "To Build White City at Lake Quinsigamond," *Worcester Evening Gazette*, March 14, 1905.

[9] Robert Goldsack, *A Century of Fun - A Pictorial History of New England Amusement Parks*, Midway Museum Publications, 1993, p. 131.

[10] "To Build White City at Lake Quinsigamond," *Worcester Evening Gazette*, March 14, 1905

[11] Undated advertising card, courtesy of Mrs. Charles Laconte.

[12] "Strike at White City," *Worcester Evening Gazette*, May 3, 1905. Also see "Orders to Bartlett," *Worcester Evening Gazette*, May 8, 1905.

[13] Ibid.

[14] Ibid.

Close to the lake was another favorite ride: the "Whirl of Captive Airships" or "Circle Swings" offered passengers a ride "over land and lake without the dangers of the real affair." (postcard, author's collection)

CIRCLE SWING. WHITE CITY. WORCESTER, MASS.

By late afternoon, a reporter visiting the site found about eighty carpenters and a large number of laborers installing various rides and attractions. The management felt confident that the strike would be of short duration and would not hinder their plans for completing the park on time.[15]

Construction proceeded smoothly until May 11, when the carpenters renewed the strike. They were upset because the management would not rehire five union carpenters who had participated in the previous strike.[16] Eventually all of the problems were worked out, but not before the opening was delayed for a number of weeks, first to the original date of May 27, then to Memorial Day, followed by June 3, June 10, and finally June 17.[17]

Even this last date, which looked promising up until the last moment, proved to be a gigantic fizzle. By this late date, many of the concessionaires had waited long enough. Each time the park was scheduled to open they hired people to work at their games and booths, only to have to let them go when the opening was postponed. When the park didn't open at the advertised time of 7 p.m. on June 17, one of these "privilege men" broke down a door at the rear of the dance pavilion and an estimated crowd of 5,000 people surged into the park.[18] When the police hired for the opening found out what happened, they formed a raiding party and began to throw out the protesting trespassers. By eight o'clock, 5,000 people were waiting outside the gate with ticket money in hand. They asked the management to open the park but the answer was still no.[19]

By 8:30 p.m. the crowd couldn't wait any longer--another door was broken down and everyone, including women and children,

surged into the dance hall. The house band, Hardy's orchestra, struck up a two-step and everyone crowded the dance floor. Once again, the police arrived. They ordered the music stopped and tossed everyone out, including several people who had escaped into the park itself.[20]

The reason the park could not open was because its temporary power plant would not work. Despite an arrangement with the Boston and Worcester trolley line to supply electric power until more permanent arrangements could be made, the much vaunted lights couldn't be lit.[21] At 9:10 p.m. the power plant fired up long enough to light some of the lights, much to the delight of the impatient patrons, but after a short time it failed completely, pitching the whole park into darkness and ending the evening. Obviously, the management had been much too optimistic in its plans to open the park by May 20.[22]

Nevertheless, the park did open the next day, June 18, a sweltering summer Sunday. The heat didn't bother the anxious crowds of pleasure seekers a bit--they crowded White City, Lincoln Park, the causeway and the surrounding area to overflowing. The only lakeside business that seemed to suffer in any way was the canoe and boat rental business. It was so hot that the sun reflecting off the water would quickly cook anyone who ventured out on the lake.[23]

All of the previous postponements of opening day at the White City amusement park were quickly forgotten by the throngs of people who rushed in when the gates opened mid-afternoon. What would become a fifty-five year adventure providing excitement and pleasure to the people of New England had begun--White City was officially open!

[15] Ibid.

[16] "Strike Renewed," *Worcester Evening Gazette,* May 11, 1905.

[17] "Break into White City," *Worcester Sunday Telegram,* June 18, 1905.

[18] Ibid.

[19] Ibid.

[20] Ibid.

[21] Ibid.

[22] Ibid.

[23] "Lake on in Full Blast," *Worcester Evening Gazette,* June 18, 1905.

Advertising cards for the first hand-cranked movies showed scenes from the movie and listed brief, catchy phrases about the story line. (both images courtesy of Brian Pierce)

The rides and other attractions were as comprehensive a package of fun and games as could possibly be imagined. A contemporary advertising brochure, printed just before the opening, gave a glowing description of the new park's features, including the "Shoot-the-Chutes," which immediately became one of the park's most popular rides.[24] Named after local towns, the ride's boats were pulled up a long incline before they zoomed down a water chute. As the boats flew down the "longest chutes east of Dreamland," they passed under an arch where people stood and watched the boats land with a giant spray of water in a man-made "Fairy Lake."[25] It was called the "Fairy Lake" because of the twice-weekly displays of fireworks and "novel, appropriate and special effects for each occasion [arranged by] Monsieur Bellodini of Paris, a Neapolitan, who has made this feature a life study."[26]

A "Miniature Railway" was just what it claimed to be: the locomotive was only five feet long and twenty-eight inches high and pulled miniature passenger cars. The engine used miniature pieces of coal and the train ran on miniature tracks. The owners even hired midgets as the conductor and the engineer. However, some of the adult passengers that squeezed on board were not miniature. The train's route wound its course throughout the park and featured "scenes of mysterious lands."[27]

Close to the lake stood another exciting favorite: the "Whirl of Captive Airships," or "Circle Swings," offered passengers a ride "over land and lake without the dangers of the real affair." Hanging from cables dangling from a tall tower, the airships spun until the passengers were "flying" over the lake.[28] This ride was updated over the years and later featured gleaming silver "rocket ships." John Cumming, who lives

in Michigan but grew up near Lake Quinsigamond, remembers this ride as much more realistic than a similar ride at Lincoln Park. "The airplanes looked like airplanes," he recalls.

An "electric show" called "Creation" claimed to show "with remarkable fidelity the biblical story of the origin of matter, the earth and man; then the flood, and later the receding of the waters and the uplifting of the budding and glorious world."[29] The "Automatic Vaudeville" penny arcade featured "all the latest mechanical wonders," including some of the first hand-cranked "movies" or "automatic living illusions."[30] Advertising cards near each machine showed a scene from the "movie" and listed brief, catchy phrases about the story line. These advertisements, many of which are part of a local collection, offer a bird's eye view into society at the time. Several were considered too risqué and stamped "Not Approved for Sunday Viewing" by local police inspectors. One example, entitled "Flirting in a Manicure Parlor," shows an old gent with a young lady sitting on his lap hugging him. The story line was easy to figure out since one of the subtitles reads, "Wifey Arrives on the Scene," and the old gent's matronly wife stands off to one side in the photo. Many other selections were not as controversial and included sports, travelogues, or current events. A sampling of titles include, "Handout Hector Helps Clean House" (Approved by New York and Chicago Censors), "A Smoke and a Smile - Frivolous Show Girls," "Demure Stenographer--You Should See What Happens" (Approved for Sunday, 1916) and "What Funny Things Girls Will Do When They Are Sweet 16."

White City's dance hall was one of its most prominent and lasting features. On the second level, a restaurant advertised to serve 1,000 people overlooked the dance floor.[31] Billed as the most beauti-

---

[24] "The White City, Lake Quinsigamond, Worcester, Massachusetts," 1907, courtesy of Michael Paika.

[25] Ibid.

[26] Ibid.

[27] Ibid.

[28] Ibid.

[29] Ibid.

[30] Ibid.

[31] "The White City, Lake Quinsigamond, Worcester, Massachusetts," 1907, courtesy of Michael Paika.

Overseeing the park was the colorful "King Dodo," a huge clown-shaped structure whose legs framed the entrance to King Dodo's Palace, also known as The Foolish House, which was similar to today's fun houses. (White City pamphlet, circa 1907, author's collection)

ful dance hall in New England, it featured the White City Orchestra and a number of its own White City songs, including "The White City Waltz Song":

I'm so lone-some sweetheart; kind of feeling blue,
Take me some-where dear-ie, where there's lots to do
Can't you think of some-place? Wist-ful-ly she sighed,
Then her tired eyes bright-ened, When her boy replied

White City's the place to go - the place where you know no care.
A dance hall like glass and the orchestra's great
The like you won't find an-y where.
There's the Scenic and Chutes or if you want a thrill,
a ride on the Air-ships take.
The place for real sport, that comes next to New York,
is White City on the Lake.[32]

A fun house area included many amusements: the "Sea on Land," had floorboards that moved and rocked as a person walked along; the popular Chilkoot Pass was a thirty-foot high slide with a hump: "More fun than you ever had before, whether you ride or watch others ride"; a hall of warped mirrors called the "Laughing Gallery"; and the "Katzenjammer Castle."[33] Another feature, a maze called "House of Trouble," prompted a "barker" to call out, "It only costs a nickel to get in, but a lot to get out!" The fun house also featured the "Fatal Wedding": "the best mirth provoking illusion show ever produced. One round of laughs."[34]

A visit to White City would not be complete without trying the carousel, observation wheel, and "Picture Gallery," where one's likeness would be transformed into a postcard ready for mailing. The Japanese Tea Garden offered a quiet place to relax from all the commotion.[35] Along the boardwalk area, or "Pike," were an array of games of chance and skill, as well as snack and drink concessions, and the mysterious "Marie Dressler's Rough House."[36] Back at the park there was a menagerie and the "Forest of Aden" for picnicking. The "Old Mill" ride followed a course around the grounds "amid scenes of tropic luxuriance and frigid grandeur."[37] Other special features included free aerial acts and fireworks displays, an athletic field and ball ground, band concerts, a garage for automobiles, space for carriages, and a boat livery on the waterfront.[38] Overseeing all was the colorful "King Dodo," a huge clown-shaped structure whose legs framed the entrance to King Dodo's Palace or The Foolish House: "[this was] a merrymaking establishment with laugh creating devices on a large scale," similar to today's fun houses.[39]

The "Custer Cars" were little go-kart type vehicles powered by small gasoline engines. These could be driven easily by all but the smallest children. White City even had its own excursion boat, appropriately named the "Miss White City," which took sightseers on trips around the lake. Later, this boat was replaced by the "New Miss White City."

The vast entertainment complex at Lake Quinsigamond was now in full swing, and White City was right at the heart of it. In the years following its opening, White City was continuously jammed with pleasure seekers. The management provided new and exciting acts regularly, many of them free. These included many wild animal

---

[32] M. H. Lewis, "The White City Waltz Song," Worcester, Mass., undated.

[33] Ibid.

[34] Ibid.

[35] Ibid.

[36] Ibid.

[37] Ibid.

[38] Ibid.

[39] Advertising booklet, 1907, author's collection.

The White City, Worcester, Mass.

The "Shoot-the-Chutes" immediately became one of the park's most popular rides. Named after local towns, the ride's boats were pulled up a long incline before they zoomed down a water chute and into the "Fairy Lake" below. (postcard, author's collection)

This brand new swimming pool took the place of the "Shoot-the-Chutes" ride during the 1920s. The pool, which was 240 feet long by 80 feet wide and cost $75,000, was said to be one of the most elaborately equipped in the country. (photo courtesy of Lucy Card)

The scenic railway (White City pamphlet, circa 1907, author's collection)

shows such as the Colonel Francis Ferrari Wild Animal Show, which featured lions and leopards.[40] Even a tame bear visited the park at one time. Gigantic fireworks displays were held from time to time: a huge extravaganza began the 1906 season.[41]

The crowds were breathless watching high wire acrobats, high divers and motorcycle daredevils. One stunt remembered by locals was performed by "Shipwreck Kelly." "Shipwreck" would climb to the top of a pole and stay there for days on end. This so intrigued the young boys in the neighborhood that at least one of them decided to try it himself and climbed up a pole in his yard. No one seems to remember how long he stayed up there, but most likely it wasn't anywhere near as long as the real "Shipwreck."

Acts came to White City from all over the country. One of the beautiful diving girls was Madeline Berlo, who had been a featured high diver at New York's Hippodrome. Photos show her in full diving show regalia, complete with an ostrich feather boa, a cape, and a diving cap. Her rhinestone-studded costume must have been scandalous then, since a good deal of the female anatomy was exposed or thinly covered.

Another popular attraction, diving horses, were recalled by Horace H. Bigelow, a grandson of the famous lake developer, in an interview with the *Sunday Telegram* in 1968: "They were handsome, pure white horses. There was a big tower rig put up for them and they'd get up there, kneel down on their front legs and dive right into the lake."[42] Since the park's managers were aware that the odd and mysterious attracted patrons, in 1907 they brought Filipino midgets to the park.[43] The Filipino midgets were a group of Igorrote Head

Hunters from the Philippine Islands who presented a complete exposition of the domestic and industrial life of the most remarkable primitive wild people of the world.[44]

One sideshow attraction was simply called "The Un-Named" and billed as "Nature's Astounding Secret--Nothing Left to Your Imagination." The rest of the advertisements are confusing: one panel read, "Children Under 18 Yrs. of Age Not Admitted." Yet another urges, "Every Mother and Daughter--Every Father and Son Should See the Un-Named." We might conclude that if the price of admission was offered, the barker would "look the other way" and most anyone could enter.

A special feature at the amusement park was the "Green Dollar Girl." White City's management hid money or "green dollar signs" adding up to $100 around the park. The *Worcester Post* reported, "The money may be hidden possibly under the benches....Possibly it will be under the seat cushion of the chute boats or scenic cars....It may be under the plates in the ice cream parlor, or under the table covers of the restaurant."[45] If a patron noticed the "Green Dollar Girl" with the green dollar sign and addressed her in the prescribed manner, the patron would receive twenty dollars in gold. The *Post* reported the proper way to address her: "'Are you the girl with the green dollar sign representing White City?' If the answer was 'Yes,' the lucky patron would have to reply, 'It belongs to me,' before receiving the prize."[46]

Horace H. Bigelow lived long enough to see his dream become a reality, but died in 1911, six years after the White City amusement park opened. His family remained associated with the park and its

---

[40] Goldsack, p. 131.

[41] Ibid.

[42] Polly Lindi, "When Venus Was Queen of the Lake," *Worcester Sunday Telegram*, August 25, 1968.

[43] *Worcester Evening Post*, July 27, 1907.

[44] Ibid.

[45] Ibid.

[46] "At White City," *Worcester Evening Post*, August 3, 1907.

Acts came to White City from all over the country. One of the beautiful diving girls was Madeline Berlo, who had been a featured high diver at New York's Hippodrome. This photo shows her in full diving show regalia, complete with an ostrich feather boa, a cape, and a diving cap. (photo, author's collection)

affairs for a number of years after his death, however. Ownership of the amusement park changed in the 1920s when George Hamid acquired a large amount of stock in the park as payment on a loan.[47] By 1927, Hamid decided to take over the park and bought out the other partners. He began to change the park's configuration and added new rides. In 1928 a giant roller coaster called the "Zip" replaced an older ride. The new coaster was built by a well known maker of amusement park rides, the Philadelphia Toboggan Company. Another feature was a new carousel from Schuykill Park in Pennsylvania. Hamid's brother Sam became manager of the park while another brother, Michele, took charge of the food concessions.[48]

A special event held at the park during the 1928 season was the Worcester County Beauty Pageant. Local beauties were anxious to be named "the most beautiful girl in Worcester County." The winner was Miss Antoinette Gualdi, a Shrewsbury girl who lived only a short distance from the park on Edgewater Avenue. She and the second and third prize winners went on tour throughout Worcester County.[49] The winner's prizes included a silver loving cup and a variety of gifts presented during personal appearances at area stores, which ranged from a "Louis Bregou Permanent Wave," to a "Famous Benrus Wrist Watch," free laundry service for thirty days, a dancing set, a nightgown and French chiffon hose. The hoopla surrounding these personal appearances fills a whole page in the August 23, 1928 edition of the *Worcester Post*.

A championship swimming meet opened the 1929 season at "Worcester's Million Dollar Playground" (White City). It was held in the brand new swimming pool that took the place of the "Shoot-the-Chutes" ride. The pool, which was 240 feet long by 80 feet wide and cost $75,000, was said to be one of the most elaborately equipped in the country. Prizes for the swimmers, "to the extent of hundreds of dollars," were provided by the park's management.[50] Admission to the new pool was thirty-five cents on weekdays and fifty cents on Sundays and holidays, a price which included admission to the park.[51] Lockers to accommodate 500 people were installed and bathing suits with the logo WCP, standing for White City Park, were available.

The park also had a new pony track for children featuring seventeen ponies, in addition to the following attractions mentioned by the local paper:

>...a miniature electric railway,...Lindy planes that sweep the water, skee ball, a novel bowling game; a "kiddie car speedway," which children under four years of age can safely operate; the "tumble bug," a rolling, swerving, novel, fun and thrill-provoking attraction; many new games, a new automatic photo gallery which takes pictures in a few minutes and completes them, and last but not least, the "fun house," a large building with novel stairs, revolving barrels, fun mirrors and other novelties.[52]

The White City amusement park weathered the Great Depression as well as could be expected. Hundreds of local people worked at White City over the years, and during the Depression it provided employment for many people. Despite hard times, by the early 1930s more improvements had been made to the park. The "Pretzel" ride and "Red Bug" ride had been installed, along with a new craze--the miniature golf course.

Angeline Perna remembers walking with her sister and two friends all the way from West Boylston to go roller skating at White

---

[47] Goldsack, p. 131.

[48] Ibid.

[49] *Worcester Evening Post*, August 23, 1928.

[50] "Swimming Meet to Dedicate New Pool," *Worcester Daily Telegram*, May 29, 1929.

[51] Ibid.

[52] Ibid.

"The Un-Named," a sideshow attraction at the amusement park (photo, author's collection)

City: "We would walk there every Sunday to go roller skating. We would only have enough money for the bus ride home, but sometimes ended up getting a ride from one of the boys that had a car."

The late Nelson Hutchinson, who was Shrewsbury's town Treasurer and Collector for many years, remembered his days working at the park in the 1920s during a 1989 interview:

> *I worked as the cashier for the roller coaster on Saturdays and Sundays from about 1920 to 1925. I would earn $2.00 for an afternoon, $4.00 on Sunday. My father was a constable for many years and spent much time from Memorial Day to Labor Day working at the park. My sister Gladys (Hutchinson) Carlson worked as the cashier at the merry-go-round.*

One fad that was popular at this time was the dance marathon. What had become the Spanish Villa Ballroom at White City hosted a number of these contests. Couples would dance for days on end with only brief rest periods, hoping to be the last ones standing, thus winning the cash prize offered for their stamina.

The Spanish Villa Ballroom, updated in 1931, became Danny Duggan's Deck, "a novel building of nautical design," in 1936. Referred to as a "mecca of thousands of dancers," it remained a popular spot for couples to dance the night away.[53] This was one of many dancing spots around the lake, which, in addition to private clubs, included the ballrooms at Lincoln Park and Winchester's on the lake, which was located approximately where the Four Season's Restaurant is today.

Just before White City's season opened in 1939, a huge fire destroyed the deck in the dance hall. The headlines read, "Maniac

May Have Set $25,000 Blaze at White City Pavilion." Shrewsbury Fire Chief Edward Logan stated, "a person mentally deficient is responsible." A nearby concession operated by John Nasif was partially destroyed with damage estimated at $4,000. Three different people reported the fire at the same time: George Fenner, who operated the boathouse on the opposite side of the turnpike from the park; Philip Johnson, a watchman at the park; and Worcester Police Officer Frank Annunziato.[54] By the time firemen arrived the dance hall was engulfed in flames. Despite the efforts of three companies of the Shrewsbury Fire Department, the deck was destroyed. An adjacent restaurant concession was heavily damaged and a number of others were reported "scorched."[55] Although threatened by the flames, the rest of the park escaped unscathed.

The Hamids were not discouraged by the fire, however, and within the next few years they made a number of improvements to White City. Joseph "Pony" Lucier of Shrewsbury worked at the park for many years. He remembers:

> *My oldest brother worked an animated game called "Walking Charlie." The object of the game was to knock "Charlie's" hat off his head to win a free cigar.*

> *It was one of fifteen games on display in the park. Four or five food stands were also opened at this time. Popcorn, ice cream, and pop, along with hot dogs and hamburgers, which sold at 5 cents – up to 10 cents – were tasty bargains.*

> *It was about this time, the Park took on a new look! When the "World's Fair" in New York ended, many things were bought and*

---

[53] Goldsack, p. 132.

[54] "Maniac May Have Set $25,000 Blaze at White City Pavilion," *Worcester Evening Gazette*, May 10, 1939.

[55] Ibid.

The popular dance hall at White City hosted various dance contests over the years and was one of the amusement park's most prominent and longest lasting attractions. (postcard, author's collection)

installed in the Park. This included new types of lighting, building fronts were changed, and a fountain 50 feet wide and 40 feet high, constructed of stainless steel and heavy glass with pretty colored lights. As water fell in a cascade from the top of the fountain it reflected all the beautiful colors of the rainbow. It was a beautiful thing to see.

Many new things were added, [including] a roller skating rink, which later became a bowling alley. A new building was constructed, where "Beano" was played for 10 cents a game. New rides were added such as the "Loop the Loop," the dark "scary" ride, rocket ride and miniature trains, and a monkey house.

...also motorboats that were situated in a pool inside the park. This same pool was previously used for swimming, and later used for housing alligators. They were used by showmen, who wrestled them. The fun house was always a big attraction. For a modest price you could stay as long as you wanted. There was a giant slide and the barrel, a spinning wheel that you could hitch a ride on — but never stayed too long because "gravity" could not hold you in place! The main attraction was an animated "Laughing Sally" outside, who always brought a laugh to everyone.

The story of the alligators mentioned by Lucier has different versions. Depending on which one you believe, one alligator or many alligators escaped into the lake. One story has them frightened by a nearby bathhouse burning; the other simply reports that an alligator escaped into the lake.

What is common to both versions of the story is that people were scared stiff! They were afraid to go swimming and went out in boats hunting for the creatures. A Shrewsbury resident who was a teenager at the time remembers going out in his uncle's boat armed with shot-guns. Some people "saw" the reptiles at points all over the lake, as far south as the area below Stringer's dam.[56] This story has two distinctly different endings, however. One tells how the alligators crawled up on shore to sun themselves and were captured by trained alligator handlers from Florida. The other tells that after the general panic died down at the end of the season, someone found a dead alligator's body in a wooded area near the roller coaster. As the story goes, the alligator died from natural causes and someone put the carcass out of the way. Whichever story you choose to believe, it is clear that there was an "alligator incident" at White City!

Pony Lucier himself ran the carousel at White City for many years. In June 1945, Carol "Candy" Paul worked at one of the nearby refreshment stands run by Michele Hamid. Although she was only fifteen at the time, she quickly learned her job: "I was able to balance eight or nine hot dogs on one arm while using the other hand to put on whatever condiments the customers wanted," Candy said.

One day Candy's older sister (she was seventeen) came by to visit, and Pony made a "pass" at her. Candy Paul wasn't happy about this and proceeded to let him know exactly how she felt. In a romantic moment they both remember to this day, their eyes met and the rest, as the saying goes, is history. Pony gave her the nickname "Candy" because of a popular song of the era that went, "I call my sugar Candy," and they began dating. Her parents were not happy about their relationship because Lucier was quite a bit older than their daughter. They soon sent Candy to far away St. Albans, Vermont to stay with an aunt for the summer, hoping the romance would cool off. Little did they know that when Candy returned on the train in August 1945 that Pony would be waiting for her at Worcester's bustling Union Station. The couple were so excited to see each other that they ran out into the busy street, almost getting run over in the process.

---

[56] Undated newspaper clipping, author's collection.

The "New Miss White City" replaced the "Miss White City" as the amusement park's excursion boat to take sightseers around the lake. (photo reprinted with permission of the Worcester Telegram & Gazette)

DO NOT
GET ON WHILE
WHEEL IS IN MOTION

This is the "barrel," a spinning wheel that you could hitch a ride on — but never stayed too long because "gravity" could not hold you in place. (photo, author's collection)

Bill's Diner, one of the many concession stands that popped up near White City amusement park as it grew in popularity. (photo, author's collection)

Theirs was a true White City romance, and three years later they were married. Another couple who worked with them at the park, Mike and Sally Vuona of Shrewsbury, stood up for them. As of 1995, the Luciers have been married for almost fifty years and have three children, thirteen grandchildren, and one great-grandchild. Wasn't there a saying, something about true love standing the test of time?

The Vuonas, now deceased, also played a part in White City's history. They invited the performers, groups like the famous trapeze act the Great Wallendas, to their house for macaroni on Sundays. Sally worked at the concessions while Mike tended to the rides, especially the "Bug," right up to the very last days of the park.

John Dunn of Boylston worked at White City in the years just before World War II. He ran two games: in one, the player would try to knock over metal milk bottles (the bottles had lead in the bottom to help keep them upright), and in the other, patrons would try to knock over dolls aligned along a board:

The best prizes were either a box of chocolate covered cherries (that cost 19 cents a box) or a maple cane with a kewpie doll on it. The least expensive were candy kisses (these cost 1/4 cent apiece). I would earn $8 a week for 12 hours work, 7 days a week, plus expense money for meals at the White City Diner. I earned enough to pay my way on our class trip to New York City and Washington DC, class photos and graduation expenses.

The White City was quite an experience in the ways of the world-- the parking lot was where a lot of people went to "park," then would come into the park. When the barkers would try to get the boyfriends to play one of the games by calling out, "Show your girlfriend what you've got!," they would sometimes answer, "I already did!"

A friend of mine ran the "Dark Ride." When one of his friends would get on the scary ride with a date, they would give him a wink.

He would flip the switch off in the middle of the ride, making sure the couple would be stranded in the dark due to a "power failure."

I would sometimes pick up pocket money by checking under the "Bug" before closing up for the night. Other times I would eat my supper, a sandwich, while riding on the roller coaster.

When Beano was introduced at White City, some women rode the bus from Worcester to play. They brought their children along and let them run wild in the park, expecting the ride operators, including Dunn, to take care of them. Dunn was not too fond of this practice and remembers that the women wouldn't leave until the last bus departed at 11 p.m. His sister, Frances (Dunn) Meleski also worked at the park. Her most vivid memories are of the performers, especially the daring high wire walkers and trapeze artists that sometimes performed at night.

Michael Perna, Sr. of Shrewsbury grew up near White City. He remembers the maintenance people preparing the park for opening day:

When I was sixteen I worked at the park for 40 cents an hour. Sometimes they had us ride on the roller coaster, just to get some weight in the cars so that the wheels would wear the rust off the tracks that got on them over the winter. At first we would go really slow and the wheels would squeak. A man would walk along a little walkway and put grease on the tracks here and there. After going around a few times the rust would begin to wear off and we would go faster and faster.

Of all the people associated with the White City amusement park during its fifty-five years of operation, the best known started off guessing people's weights. Today, David "Duddie" Massad is a successful businessman in the area. He worked at White City for a number of years before World War II, and later he became involved in the park's management.

Overhead view of a crowd at White City, circa 1929
Notice the Fun House on the left and "The Whip" ride on the right. (photo courtesy of Lucy Card)

On "The Whip" at White City (photo, author's collection)

Michael Vuona is standing near the entrance to Kiddie Land at the White City amusement park.
The roller coaster is in the background. He and his wife both worked at the park for many years.
(photo courtesy of Dorothy Skiest)

During the war years, the park was a haven for the war-weary populace. It was a place where people went to forget the troubled times. Even unpleasant times, when "blackouts" were enforced and a serviceman was killed while standing up on the roller coaster, couldn't put the damper on the White City for long. The park was a favorite place where servicemen home on leave enjoyed themselves with their sweethearts. Pony Lucier recalls, "...I still can hear the sound of the pipe organ and the sound of people laughing and enjoying themselves in a very unsettled, tense world. We were at war, and people needed to unwind and have fun."

When the war was over, White City was soon going full tilt. Dance contests again became popular. Returning servicemen were only too happy to dance with females after spending time overseas in combat, usually exclusively in male company. According to Robert Goldsack in his book, *A Century of Fun - A Pictorial History of New England Amusement Parks*, the Hamids spent $100,000 sprucing up the park grounds and rebuilding the fun house after the war. Goldsack also notes that in his autobiography, George Hamid tells how he avoided losing the park to mortgage holders during a financial crisis: "Knowing that he would be served with papers at a certain time, Hamid had all the clocks in the park set back one hour, giving him the necessary time to scrape together the cash needed to cover the overdue payment."

Over the years, many other businesses sprung up in the area of White City. No less than four diners catered to the crowds. Nightclubs and bars clustered around the park: Tilli's, the Happy Hour, Bronzo's and the Palais Royale. The Happy Hour, operated by the Santello family, was well known for hosting famous Hollywood stars. Life-size pictures of some of them were displayed on the walls. Albert "Lovey" Garganigo remembers spending "one memorable night" at The Happy Hour in the company of the beautiful movie star, Jane Russell.

The next transition in the history of the White City amusement park took place in 1954, when the park was bought by a real estate developer from New York, Irwin Knohl. In what appeared to be a very strange business arrangement, Irwin's father Larry Knohl took charge of the park's management and a rapid expansion began.[57] Larry Knohl himself was quite a character. A recent *New England Real Estate Journal* article describes him:

> *He was a New Yorker with a colorful past which included an association with Frank Costello, James Hoffa, and T. Lamar Caudle, former head of the Justice Department's Tax Division, who resigned at the request of President Truman. Knohl's business activities ranged from operation of a used car lot to restaurants to ownership of the General Oglethorpe Hotel in Georgia. He had served time for embezzlement and was questioned in the 1957 slaying of Murder, Inc.'s Albert Anastasia.[58]*

A colorful past, indeed! No wonder the business was purchased in his son's name. Problems arose within a short time. The park's management wanted to install pinball machines in the arcade. At the time, these machines were banned in many cities and towns throughout the state, including Worcester, because they promoted gambling.[59] A furor arose because people from Worcester and Shrewsbury objected to licensed pinball machines in Shrewsbury. Shrewsbury's Board of Selectmen, advised by the police department that the games were legal, had granted a license to operate pinball machines and other coin operated machines in the arcade. The board had received assurances from Charles Hamid (who was still associated with the park) and Larry Knohl (who denied owning the park) that there would be no gambling associated with the machines; the board members even visited the park. Nevertheless, the Board of Selectmen asked the police department to supervise the park to insure that no

[57] Goldsack, p. 132. Also see *New England Real Estate Journal*, June 2-8, 1995.

[58] *New England Real Estate Journal*, June 2-8, 1995.

[59] "Police To Scan Pinball Play at White City," *Worcester Evening Gazette*, May 27, 1955. Also see "51 Machines Licensed at White City," *Worcester Evening Gazette*, May 31, 1955.

Joseph "Pony" Lucier is standing on the carousel at White City. Lucier worked at the park and operated the carousel for many years. (photo courtesy of Joseph "Pony" Lucier)

gambling took place.[60] The local papers didn't like the decision either. The *Evening Gazette* offered the following opinion:

> The issue is not whether the operation of such machines can be made legal by licensing. Obviously, it can. Rather, the matter involves these questions: Do such machines make gambling easy? Are they particularly attractive to those who can least afford to throw away money on them? Do they often open the door to graft and racketeering?
>
> We cannot answer those questions for Shrewsbury. Only the people of the town can do that. But we know the answer in one community after another that has had experience with pinball machines: a loud and unhappy "Yes."[61]

In the end the pinballs stayed, having little or no adverse effect on the local citizenry.

In 1955, the adjacent Bigelow estate, where Horace H. Bigelow had lived, was purchased. This added eight and a half acres to the park for picnic grounds, a 2,000-foot beach and additional parking space.[62] Other planned improvements included a new fun house, a ferris wheel, a roll-o-plane ride, a monkey "park," an eighteen hole miniature golf course, a large ballroom, swanboats and some new kiddie rides. The carousel was moved to the corner of the Boston Turnpike and South Quinsigamond Avenue. The old bowling alley was torn down and replaced by a new brick building used to house games and refreshment concessions.[63]

Also in 1955, construction of a new roller coaster began (the previous one had been torn down in 1951).[64] It would be 2,480 feet long and have a 73-foot drop. By February 1956, 125 feet of the ride had been

erected rising 40 feet into the air. However, a severe windstorm on February 25 blew the whole structure down, leaving nothing but a heap of twisted rubble. The falling debris toppled telephone poles along South Quinsigamond Avenue, knocking out power to about 600 families. Fortunately this happened at night, otherwise many people on this busy street might have been killed or injured.[65] Damages amounted to about $30,000, none of which was covered by insurance. Larry Knohl assured everyone that the coaster would be built according to the original plans, at a total cost of $130,000. Before the roller coaster could be rebuilt, seven new rides were installed: the Spinaroo, Tub of Fun, Race Horse, Twirl-a-Whirl, Stage Coach, Motorcycle Track, and Hot Rod Track.[66]

The park's management continued to bring in acts to help promote the park. Among the stars appearing over the years were Bobby Darin, Edie Gorme, Paul Anka, Jerry Vale, The Four Coins, The Four Aces, The Four Lads, Frankie Avalon, and television personality Dagmar. Despite such efforts to keep the park going, it steadily declined. Sadly, the 1960 season would be White City's last. In fifty-five years, the park had entertained as many as 40,000 people in one day and brought much happiness to millions more. On Labor Day 1960 the White City amusement park closed forever.

On November 12, 1961, the *Boston Globe* interviewed sixty-seven-year-old White City caretaker Arthur Johnson, who had worked at the park for thirty-three years, living in three small rooms at the back of what was once the bowling alley. After reminiscing about the huge crowds that once swarmed the park, Johnson mused:

> The real sadness was slowly watching the thousands that came on Sundays and holidays dwindle down to a handful. The park was beginning to become a lonely place...the children were gone.

---

60 Ibid.

61 "Shrewsbury Selectmen and the 40 Pinballs," *Worcester Evening Gazette*, June 1, 1955.

62 "White City Buys Estate in order to Expand," *Worcester Telegram*, January 5, 1955.

63 Ibid.

64 "Backstage With James Lee," *Worcester Evening Gazette*, February 29, 1956. Also see Goldsack, p. 132.

65 "Backstage With James Lee," *Worcester Evening Gazette*, February 29, 1956.

66 Ibid.

Into the pool at White City – notice the letters WC on the women's bathing suits; the letters stand for White City. (photo, author's collection)

The gray man winces at the sound of another building that once was gaudy and glamorous being reduced by the wreckers. (The caretaker wiped his eyes with a "wrinkled hand" and looked at his companion, a German Shepard named "King") Where can a man 67 years old go? Maybe I will move into the city somewhere. But what would I do with King? I've had an offer to work as a carpenter at a drive-in. Maybe I can go there. With all this going on around me, I don't know what to do. (As the old caretaker looked out over the piles of rubble he said,) "I'll stay right here until they tear the walls down around me."

Another, more eloquent account quoted the old caretaker: "I've seen it come and now I've seen it go; it was the queen of them all."[67]

It would not be a peaceful ending, however: a string of mysterious fires would consume most of this venerable pleasure palace before all was said and done. In the fall of 1960 a nearby diner went up in flames. The next day, evidence revealed a failed attempt to burn the bowling alleys at Lincoln Park. Within the next week or two, a shed in the rear of Bronzo's Restaurant burned, followed by Fenner's boathouse. Then a number of summer cottages near the park burned down in November.[68] In April 1961, an unsuccessful attempt was made to burn the outdoor stage at White City by placing mattresses up against it and setting them on fire. The Lakeside Ballroom at Lincoln Park burned down the following month. Evidence of arson was found at every site, according to both the State Fire Marshall's office and the Shrewsbury Fire Department.[69]

On May 23, 1961 fire struck the White City again. In a spectacular, fast burning blaze, the fun house burned to the ground and the nearby shooting gallery and caterpillar ride were damaged. The fire, discovered by a passerby shortly after 11 p.m., was out of control by the time fire-fighters arrived. Despite the efforts of about fifty firefighters who poured 100,000 gallons of water on the blaze, the building was totally destroyed.[70] By directing streams of water at three sides of the fun house from the roofs of adjacent buildings, the firemen were able to keep the fire from spreading any further.[71]

On November 1, 1961, the White City amusement park was sold at an auction for $385,000. Various rides, buildings and other fixtures fetched roughly $40,000 more. This sale was complicated by the Federal Bureau of Internal Revenue agents from Brooklyn, New York and Boston, Massachusetts, which served two liens totaling $501,717 at the time of the auction. An assessment totaling $494,000 had been made earlier "against the park and a person holding a financial interest in the park." This person was identified as Larry Knohl, and the lien was an attempt by the federal government to collect income taxes.[72] Knohl had been charged with income tax evasion in 1949 and 1950 and found not guilty. He had also been indicted on federal charges for stock manipulation.[73]

Albert Shore of Providence, Rhode Island, who held a mortgage on the park, was the high bidder at the auction. His plans for the property were to develop it into a shopping center, a motel, or a discount house.[74] Since Shore's bid had not received approval from Larry Knohl, who was still listed as the owner of the park, White City's final days would linger until the spring of 1962. This delay didn't prevent the defunct park from being struck by fire one more time before the sale was final. Over the winter another huge, set blaze burned the building that housed the roller skating rink and bowling alley to the ground.[75]

A casualty of this inferno was the giant sign that had flashed a neon

---

[67] Goldsack, p. 133.

[68] "Fire at White City Termed Suspicious," *Worcester Evening Gazette*, May 23, 1961.

[69] Ibid.

[70] "White City Fun House Burns," *Worcester Telegram*, May 23, 1961.

[71] Ibid.

[72] "White City Park Sold at Auction," *Worcester Telegram*, November 2, 1961. Also see "White City Site Sold for $200,000," *Worcester Telegram*, March 27, 1962.

[73] Ibid.

[74] Ibid.

[75] "More of White City Leveled by 'Set' Fire," *Worcester Telegram*, February 12, 1962.

A gleaming silver rocket ship carried passengers over land and lake on the "Whirl of Captive Airships"/ "Circle Swings" ride. (photo reprinted with permission of the Worcester Telegram & Gazette)

"WHITE CITY" to the surrounding area for many years. This sign, along with the building, had been sold during the November 1961 auction. A Mr. Arthur Peckham, the operator of the Roger Park Zoo in Wisconsin, bought the building and the sign for $400. He wanted to display the sign at the zoo. Shrewsbury town officials weren't sure why Peckham hadn't moved the sign by the time of the fire, but felt that he was probably waiting for warmer weather before undertaking the move.[76]

This fire was discovered at 12:10 a.m. by an off-duty Shrewsbury firefighter, Private Michael Perna, Sr., who had stopped at a nearby diner for a midnight snack. As Perna and his wife were leaving the diner he noticed the rolling flames and went back into the diner to call the fire department. By the time firefighters arrived, the building was an inferno and the huge sign "toppled with a mighty roar soon after," according to the local papers. A witness said, "[the sign] just sank down inside the building, like a drowning swimmer."[77]

At the height of the fire, flames shot more than fifty feet in the air. The firemen were hampered by the sub-zero cold, but even this didn't prevent hundreds of people from gathering to watch. A nearby supermarket parking lot filled up with spectators, like "a drive-in theater," Private Perna described.[78] One of those spectators was his wife, Angeline. She recalls, "It got so hot from the flames that I had to keep backing the car up. After a while, I decided to go home and figured he would call if he needed a ride. He came home later but had ruined the suit he was wearing and then ended up with pneumonia."

The next day the once brilliant beacon of White City lay on its side in the ruins, covered with ice from the water sprayed on the fire, a sad reminder of a glorious past. The once great White City was no more. The crowds of people seeking the rides and games, the fun house and the sideshow attractions were gone too. With the park's

passing, an era had truly ended at Lake Quinsigamond.

The following March, Albert Shore demanded a foreclosure auction. The park sold for $200,000, a price which included the land and one remaining building.[79] By the following year, Shore had built one of the first shopping centers in the area, with a Bradlee's department store, a supermarket and a number of smaller stores. Within a few years, a movie theater was also built.

Today all that remains of the great amusement park are a few rusting steel beams, remnants of the wharves at White City's beach. The White City name was retained for the shopping plaza, and later included "White City East" when more stores were built on the other side of South Quinsigamond Avenue. Today many people don't make a connection between the shopping center's name and the amusement park.

One last story illustrates just how popular the White City amusement park was, even after it had been closed and the shopping center was built. Eleanor Shea, who grew up near the lake, worked at a doughnut shop at the White City shopping complex. One day, a woman came into the shop, leaving a car full of children parked outside. She looked somewhat bewildered, as people sometimes do when they are looking for a place they think they should have reached. The woman asked Mrs. Shea for directions to the White City amusement park. She was sure it was nearby, and she had traveled all the way from Lynn, Massachusetts with her children to visit the park. Sadly, Mrs. Shea told the woman that she was standing on what was left of the White City amusement park.

---

[76] Ibid.

[77] Ibid.

[78] Ibid.

[79] "White City Sold for $200,000," *Worcester Telegram*, March 27, 1962.

Different games offered a variety of prizes to winners: chocolate covered cherries, cigars, candy kisses, and maple canes with kewpie dolls on them. (photo, author's collection)

When the White City amusement park closed in 1960 and was subsequently sold, the huge entertainment complex on Lake Quinsigamond's shores had almost entirely vanished. Though a few of the old social clubs and beaches remained, one by one they closed too, until the lake was only a shadow of its former self.

Small reminders of more peaceful and pleasant days at the lake can be found in a number of small private collections. One incudes tiny teacups and saucers with scenes of the old lake printed on them, as well as "flash glass" items with "White City, Worcester, Mass." etched into the cranberry colored glass, and a variety of paper memorabilia.

Another collection belongs to Michael Paika, who has to be one of, if not the most enthusiastic "lake person" around. Michael not only lives on the lake, but he owns Blake Island too. The centerpiece of his collection of Lake Quinsigamond artifacts is an antique scale that was used to verify weights at a weight-guessing booth at White City. Glass display cases on both sides of the scale were used to display prizes.

A possible link to White City's past, yet unproven, can be found in Syracuse, New York at a shopping mall called the Carousel Center, which contains an old carousel. A partially documented history of this ride states that it was once used in Worcester, MA, among other locations. This may be the carousel from Lincoln Park or possibly an early White City ride, since White City's carousel was replaced in the late 1920s. The Pyramid Companies that own the carousel have been very cooperative in trying to trace its history, although with no success to date.

Some of the lake's mysteries may be solved by future historians. The string of fires that destroyed much of White City, one of the premier amusement areas in New England, if not the country, remain a mystery. Some were accidental but the majority were not. Maybe the owners of the buildings wanted to collect insurance money; perhaps a pyromaniac was on the loose; or possibly a disgruntled customer or employee held a grudge against the management.

Of course, a work of this type can never be completely finished. Other bits and pieces of Lake Quinsigamond's history will continue to pop up, probably as soon as this edition is printed. I hope that more interesting Lake Quinsigamond stories will come to light!

On November 1, 1961, the White City amusement park was sold at an auction for $385,000 to Albert Shore. Shore wanted to develop the property into a shopping center, a motel, or a discount house. (photo reprinted with permission of the Worcester Telegram & Gazette)

Carlson, Stephen P. and Thomas W. Harding. *Worcester Trolleys Remembered*. Worcester Regional Transit Authority, 1985.

Fiske, Edward R. *Pleasure Resorts in Worcester County*. Worcester, Mass., 1877.

Goldsack, Robert. *A Century of Fun - A Pictorial History of New England Amusement Parks*. Nashua, NH: Midway Museum Publications, 1993.

Nourse, W.J.H., Ed. "The Tatassit Totem," undated.

Nutt, Charles, A.B. *History of Worcester and Its People*. New York: Lewis Historical Publishing Co., 1919.

Quinsigamond Boat Club. *The Quinsigamond Boat Club of Worcester, Massachusetts, 1857-1917*. Worcester, Mass., 1917.

The Railroad Commission. *The Town of Shrewsbury, Massachusetts, U.S.A. - It's Location, Advantages and Attractions as a Place of Residence and for Business*. Shrewsbury, Mass., 1890.

Rice, Franklin P. *Dictionary of Worcester (Massachusetts) and Its Vicinity*. Worcester: F.S. Blanchard & Co., 1889.

Worcester Consolidated Street Railway Company. *Picturesque Views on & Adjacent to the Routes of the Worcester Consolidated Street Railway and at Lake Quinsigamond*. Worcester, 1898.

Other publications by Chandler House Press,
A division of Tatnuck Bookseller & Sons:

• •

Tornado! 84 Minutes, 94 Lives
by John M. O'Toole

Tornado in New England Video
by Marvin Richmond

Once-Told Tales of Worcester County
by Albert B. Southwick

More Once-Told Tales of Worcester County
by Albert B. Southwick

Favorite Places of Worcester County
by Larry Abramoff, Gloria Abramoff & Ann Lindblad

The Worcester Account
by S. N. Behrman

Affirmations of Wealth: 101 Secrets of Daily Success
by V. John Alexandrov

*A Woman Doctor's Guide to Hormone Therapy:
How to Choose What's Right for You*
by Nananda Francette Col, MD

150 Years of Worcester: 1848-1998
by Albert B. Southwick

Vintage Worcester, Massachusetts
poster, puzzle, post cards & post card book

to order any of the items listed above or additional copies of
Remembering Lake Quinsigamond: From Steamboats to White City
by Michael P. Perna, Jr.

please contact
Chandler House Press
335 Chandler Street, Worcester, MA 01602
(800) 642-6657
(508) 756-9425 Fax
www.tatnuck.com

Coming in Spring/Summer 1998 from Chandler House Press

For All Our Daughters:
How Mentoring Helps Young Women and Girls Master the Art of
Growing Up
by Pegine Echevarria

Golf for Everybody:
A Lifetime Guide for Learning, Playing and Enjoying the Game
by Brad Brewer, Director of the Worldwide Arnold Palmer Golf
Academies and Steve Hosid, Instruction Editor of the PGA Tour's
Partners magazine

The Power of Will:
Key Strategies to Unlock Your Inner Strengths
and Enjoy Success in All Aspects of Life
by Anthony Parinello

Successful Business Networking
by Frank De Raffele, Jr. and Edward D. Hendricks

The Woman's Fix-It Book:
Incredibly Simple Weekend Projects and Everyday Home Repair
by Karen Dale Dustman

The Titan Principle: The #1 Secret to Sales Success
by Ron Karr

Your People Are Your Product:
How to Hire the Best So You Can Stay the Best
by Don Blohowiak

for more information, contact
Chandler House Press
335 Chandler Street, Worcester, MA 01602
(800) 642-6657
(508) 756-9425 Fax
www.tatnuck.com